D0085486

Portraits of Coleridge

I. Moses Haughton

Portraits of Coleridge

MORTON D. PALEY

OXFORD
UNIVERSITY PRESS
Great Clarendon Street, Oxford OX2 6DP

Oxford University Press is a department of the University of Oxford.
It furthers the University's objective of excellence in research, scholarship,
and education by publishing worldwide in

Oxford New York

Athens Auckland Bangkok Bogotá Buenos Aires Cape Town
Chennai Dar es Salaam Delhi Florence Hong Kong Istanbul Karachi
Kolkata Kuala Lumpur Madrid Melbourne Mexico City Mumbai Nairobi
Paris São Paulo Shanghai Singapore Taipei Tokyo Toronto Warsaw

and associated companies in Berlin Ibadan

Oxford is a registered trade mark of Oxford University Press
in the UK and in certain other countries

Published in the United States
by Oxford University Press Inc., New York

Reprinted 2001

ISBN 0-19-818469-7

Printed in Great Britain
on acid-free paper by
Bookcraft (Bath) Short Run Books
Midsomer Norton

TO THE OWNERS OF THE PORTRAITS,
PUBLIC AND PRIVATE,
WHOSE GENEROUS CO-OPERATION
HAS MADE THIS BOOK POSSIBLE

Acknowledgements

In the course of my research for this book I have contracted intellectual debts which are a pleasure to acknowledge. For intellectual stimulation and invaluable advice I am indebted to J. C. C. Mays, Tim Fulford, Martin Butlin, and Carl Woodring. Without their help *Portraits of Coleridge* would have remained a mere idea, and their generosity can only be repaid by being passed on by its recipient to other scholars in the future.

Permission to reproduce pictures was kindly given by the owners credited in the List of Illustrations. I am also grateful to the following individuals and institutions for assisting my work: N. F. Plumley, Dot Mariner, and Christ's Hospital; Kai Kin Yung, Ian Ritchie, and the National Portrait Gallery; Robert Woof and the Wordsworth Museum, Grasmere; Nigel Lacey and Jesus College, Cambridge; Alistair Laing and The National Trust; Lynne Miller and the Wedgwood Museum; Christine Reynolds and Westminster Abbey; Virginia Murray and John Murray, Publishers, Ltd.; Frances Carey and the Department of Prints and Drawings of the British Museum; Linda Stanley and the Historical Society of Pennsylvania; Jennie Rathbun and the Houghton Library; Tim Schadla-Hall and the Leicestershire Museums; M. H. Kaufman and the Henderson Trust Collection of the University of Edinburgh; Tim Hoyer and the Bancroft Library; Michaelyn Burnette and the Library of the University of California at Berkeley; V. Partington and Sotheby's; Gwynyyd Gosling and the Highgate Scientific and Literary Institution; Leslie Wearb and the Harry Ransom Center for Research in the Humanities of the University of Texas at Austin.

The colour plates were made possible by the generosity of the Paul Mellon Centre for Studies in British Art.

I wish especially to express appreciation for the research

opportunities given me by the British Library, the Department of Prints and Drawings of the British Museum, the Department of Prints and Drawings of the Victoria and Albert Museum, the Henry E. Huntington Library and Art Gallery, the New York Public Library, the Columbia University Libraries, the National Art Collections Library at the Victoria and Albert Museum, the National Portrait Gallery Archive, and the Libraries of the University of California at Berkeley.

For particular information and other courtesies I am grateful to Joan Coleridge, Denise Coleridge, G. W. C. Coleridge, Mary Coleridge, Lord Coleridge, Sir Charles and Lady Cave, V. Gardner, Walter B. Crawford, Jonathan Wordsworth, Shelley Bennett, Eric Nye, David Bindman, Robert N. Essick, David Blayney Brown, Grevel Lindop, William Levine, Tom Mayberry, Detlef W. Dörrbecker, Reggie Waters, and Sarah McKibben.

My work was generously supported by annual grants from the Chancellor's Office and the Committee on Research of the University of California, Berkeley. Helen Oless, Beverly Scherf, and John Ives contributed much-needed help at the Berkeley English Department, as did Ursula Otto and Peter Schneider at the Englisches Seminar of the University of Zürich. At Oxford University Press I benefited from the encouragement and advice of Jason Freeman and Sophie Goldsworthy and from the editorial assistance of Janet Moth and Sylvia Jaffrey. Thanks to an invitation from Nicholas Roe I had the stimulus of presenting my preliminary research at the International Coleridge Conference.

Last and first, the confidence in this project of my wife, Gunnel Tottie, enabled me to bring it to completion.

M.D.P.

Zürich
27 July 1998

Contents

List of Illustrations

Abbreviations

BL	British Library
BL	S. T. Coleridge, *Biographia Literaria*
BM	British Museum
CC	Collected Coleridge
C & L	W. B. Crawford and E. S. Lauterbach, *Samuel Taylor Coleridge: Annotated Bibliography*, ii.
CL	S. T. Coleridge, *Collected Letters*
CN	*The Notebooks of Samuel Taylor Coleridge*, ed. K. Coburn *et al.*
CPW	S. T. Coleridge, *Complete Poetical Works*
Crawford	*Samuel Taylor Coleridge: Annotated Bibliography*, iii.
DC	Derwent Coleridge
Dict.	A. Graves, *Dictionary of Artists Who Have Exhibited Works in the Principal London Exhibitions from 1760 to 1893*
EHC	Ernest Hartley Coleridge
EY	William and Dorothy Wordsworth, *Letters: The Early Years*
Haven	R. Haven, J. Haven, and M. Adams, *Samuel Taylor Coleridge: Annotated Bibliography*, i.
HEH	The Henry E. Huntington Library and Art Gallery
HLSI	Highgate Literary and Scientific Association
HNC	Henry Nelson Coleridge
HRC	Harry Ransom Humanities Research Center
LY	William and Dorothy Wordsworth, *Letters: The Later Years*
MY	William and Dorothy Wordsworth, *Letters: The Middle Years*
NPG	National Portrait Gallery
NYPL	New York Public Library
RA	Royal Academy
Royal Academy	A. Graves, *The Royal Academy*
RP	R. Walker, *Regency Portraits*
SC	Sara Coleridge
TLS	*Times Literary Supplement*
TT	Samuel Taylor Coleridge, *Table Talk*

A Coleridge Chronology

1772	(21 Oct.) Born at Ottery St Mary, Devon; (13 Dec.) baptized at the church of St Mary
1781	Death of father, Revd John Coleridge
1782	(Sept.)–1791 Studies at Christ's Hospital, London
1791	(Sept.)–1793 (Dec.) Studies at Jesus College, Cambridge
1793	(2 Dec.) Enlists in the Light Dragoons
1794	(Apr.) Returns to Cambridge; meets Robert Southey in Oxford
	(Aug.) Meets Thomas Poole; engaged to Sara Fricker
	The Fall of Robespierre (written with Southey) published
	(Dec.) Leaves Cambridge
	(24 Dec.) Begins writing *Religious Musings*
1795	Bristol: Political lectures and lectures on revealed religion
	Vandyke portrait
	(Oct.) Marries Sara Fricker
	Pantisocracy project given up
	Meets William Wordsworth
1796	*The Watchman*
	(Apr.) *Poems on Various Subjects*
	Hancock portrait
1797	(Oct.) *Poems*; completes *Osorio*
	(Nov.) Begins *Ancient Mariner*
1798	Wedgwood annuity
	(Mar.) *France: An Ode*
	(Apr.) *Fears in Solitude*
	Shuter portrait
	(Sept.) *Lyrical Ballads*; to Germany with William and Dorothy Wordsworth
1798/9	**German** portrait
1799	(Feb.) At Göttingen
	(July) Returns to Nether Stowey
	(Oct.) Travels in the Lake District with Wordsworth; meets Sara Hutchinson
1800	(Jan.–Apr.) *Morning Post* journalism
	Translates *Wallenstein*
	(July) Moves to Keswick

1801	*Lyrical Ballads*, with *Preface*
	Morning Post journalism
1802	(Apr.) *Dejection*, original version
	John Hazlitt portrait
	(23 Dec.) Sara Coleridge born
1803	*Poems*
	Meets Sir George and Lady Beaumont
	William Hazlitt sketch and portrait
	(Aug.) Tour of Scotland with William and Dorothy Wordsworth
1804	**Dance** portrait
	Northcote portrait
	(Apr.) Departs for Malta
1805	At Malta
	(Sept.–Dec.) In Italy
1806	(Jan.) Meets Washington Allston in Rome
	First **Allston** portrait
	(17 Aug.) Arrives in England
1806	(21 Dec.)–1807 With William Wordsworth, Dorothy Wordsworth, and Sara Hutchinson at Coleorton; hears Wordsworth read *The Prelude*
	'To William Wordsworth'
1807	(Aug.) Meets Thomas De Quincey
1808	Lectures at Royal Institution on poetry and principles of taste
	(Jan.–June) In London, writes for the *Courier*
	(Sept.) Lives with the Wordsworths at Allan Bank, Grasmere, apart from his wife
	Betham portrait
1809	(1 June) *The Friend* begins publication
1810	(Mar.) Sara Hutchinson leaves for Wales
	(15 Mar.) Last issue of *The Friend*
	(Oct.) Coleridge and Wordsworth quarrel
	In London
1811	Writes for the *Courier*
	(18 Nov.) Begins lectures on Shakespeare and Milton
	Dawe portrait and life-mask
1812	Reissuing of *The Friend*
	Dawe bust
	(Nov.)–1813 (Jan.) lectures on Shakespeare
1814	Bristol lectures on literature
	Second **Allston** portrait
1815	Dictates the *Biographia Literaria*

1816	(Apr.) Moves to Highgate to live with the Gillmans
	Leslie portrait
	Christabel, *Kubla Khan*, and *The Pains of Sleep*
	The Statesman's Manual
1817	*Biographia Literaria* and *Sibylline Leaves*
1818	Second **Leslie** portrait
	Phillips portrait begun (completed 1821)
	(Dec.)–1819 (Mar.) Lectures on philosophy and on literature
1823	Moves with the Gillmans to 3 The Grove, Highgate
1825	*Aids to Reflection*
	Delivers lecture 'On the *Prometheus* of Aeschylus'
	Spurzheim takes life-mask
1826	**De Predl** portrait
1828	Tours Netherlands and the Rhine with William and Dora Wordsworth
	Poetical Works
1829	*On the Constitution of the Church and State*
1830	*The Devil's Walk* published with Southey as co-author
1832	**Haughton** portrait
1833	**Kayser** portrait
	Maclise portrait
	Wivell portrait
1834	(25 June) Dies at Highgate

I

Introduction: The Image of the Romantic Poet

On 10–11 May 1817 John Keats wrote to his friend the artist Benjamin Robert Haydon:

When in the Isle of W<h>ight I met with a Shakespeare in the Passage of the House at which I lodged—it comes nearer to my idea of him than any I have seen.—I was but there a Week yet the old Woman made me take it with me though I went off in a hurry—Do you not think this is ominous of good?[1]

Keats has recontextualized and internalized the image of Shakespeare in the engraving—probably after the Chandos portrait[2]—so that it becomes an icon of his own poetic destiny, a 'good genius' or 'Presider', as he puts it in the same letter. Here we see one of the roles the portrait of a poet can assume for the Romantic imagination. Of course it can have far more ordinary functions. 'When you look upon a portrait,' wrote Samuel Taylor Coleridge, 'you must not compare it with the face when present, but with the recollection of the face. It refers not so much to the senses, as to the ideal sense of the friend not present.'[3] In such a role, the portrait of a poet functions for its contemporary viewers much as any other portrait of a friend or loved one. Yet for us who come after, it serves different purposes. Although we may not invest such a portrait with the intensity of meaning that

[1] *The Letters of John Keats 1814–1821*, ed. Hyder Edward Rollins (Cambridge, Mass.: Harvard University Press, 1958), i. 141–2.

[2] See David Piper, *The English Face*, 2nd edn. (London: NPG, 1992), 60. The Chandos portrait (NPG), attributed to John Taylor and dated *c.*1610, is reproduced as pl. 49.

[3] *Lectures 1808–1819 on Literature*, CC 5, ed. R. A. Foakes (2 vols.; Princeton: Princeton University Press, 1987), i. 225.

Keats did his Presider, it is for us a document in the poet's biography; and indeed a sequence of such portraits themselves constitute a biography. They are also revealing about the assumptions not only of the subject and the artist but also those of the culture to which they belong. The twenty-four portraits of Coleridge known to have been taken during the poet's lifetime[4] have much to tell us, and the posthumous and imaginary ones compose an interesting postscript. Before we turn to these, we should consider the tradition of portraiture of which they form a part.

During the eighteenth century, the living poet most represented in all media in Britain was Alexander Pope. The celebrated depiction attributed to Jonathan Richardson (NPG)[5] indicates the subject's vocation by crowning him profusely with laurel, a piece of iconography that links the Augustan poet to the classical world. A different approach is taken in Godfrey Kneller's rendering of Pope in a meditative pose, his eyes reflecting light from an unseen source, his head supported by his right hand, his elbow on a copy of Homer.[6] Such a posture was also utilized by Jean van Loo, who also placed a manuscript in the poet's left hand and raised his luminous gaze slightly upward.[7] Such attention to the poet's eye and gaze became increasingly pronounced during the eighteenth century, as we can see in Sir Joshua Reynolds's 1756 portrait of Samuel Johnson (NPG).[8] That this is principally the author of *The Vanity of Human Wishes* rather than of the *Dictionary* is attested by the lack of books or any other lexicographic equipment. (David Piper notes that a dictionary

[4] This figure includes lost portraits but does not include replicas or portraits not taken from life.

[5] This and other pictures of Pope are discussed in William Kurtz Wimsatt, *The Portraits of Alexander Pope* (New Haven and London: Yale University Press, 1965). For the Richardson portrait, see pp. 217–20 and the colour pl. facing p. 137.

[6] See Wimsatt, *Portraits of Alexander Pope*, 60–2. The picture is reproduced facing p. 60.

[7] The two original versions of this portrait are discussed and reproduced by Wimsatt, *Portraits of Alexander Pope*, 315–19.

[8] Reproduced by David Piper in *The Image of the Poet: British Poets and Their Portraits* (Oxford: Clarendon, 1982), fig. 95.

volume and other objects were later painted in and were removed in 1977.)[9] There is only a pen in the subject's right hand and paper under his left. He sprawls Ursa Major-like in his chair, his bright eyes looking into a distance that is not physical. Such an emphasis on the eyes becomes even more intense later in the century in a representation of the poet that is not a portrait at all.

In 1775, John Hamilton Mortimer exhibited at the Society of Arts a series of drawings of characters from Shakespeare, and he subsequently issued twelve etchings after them. One of these, entitled *Poet*, became especially celebrated. The passage illustrated is the famous one spoken by Theseus in *A Midsummer-Night's Dream*:

> The poet's eye, in a fine frenzy rolling,
> Doth glance from heaven to earth, from earth to heaven;
> And as imagination bodies forth
> The forms of things unknown, the poet's pen
> Turns them to shapes and gives to airy nothing
> A local habitation and a name.[10]

The Poet, unlike the other figures Mortimer depicted, is not a fictitious character but a projection from the imagery of the text.[11] This archetypal poet displays features found in portraits previously discussed. Laurel-crowned, his lips parted in breathless anticipation, he glances upward to his left. In his left eye a highlight produces the effect of a gleam, one that the viewer does not imagine to reflect natural light. That gleam reappears in one of the finest portraits of a later eighteenth-century poet, George Romney's pastel of William Cowper (NPG). The link was made explicit by William Hayley, a friend of both the artist and the poet: 'Romney wished to express what he often saw in studying the features of Cowper: "*The poet's eye in a fine frenzy rolling.*" '[12]

[9] Ibid. 92.

[10] v. i. 12–17. The lines inscribed under the print differ in minor ways from the text as given here.

[11] See John Sunderland, *John Hamilton Mortimer: His Life and Works* (London: The Walpole Society, 1988), 80. The picture is reproduced as pl. 160.

[12] William Hayley, *The Life of George Romney, Esq.* (Chichester, 1809), 178, 181. The portrait is reproduced by David Piper in *The English Face*, 2nd edn., ed. Malcolm Rogers (London: NPG, 1992), pl. 166.

When William Blake came to engrave a frontispiece for Hayley's biography of Cowper, he accentuated the gleam and placed it in both eyes.[13] A further history of this visionary gleam would include the only commissioned portrait of Blake himself, painted by Thomas Phillips in 1806 (NPG). According to an anecdote related by Allan Cunningham, Phillips stimulated Blake to assume what might be considered a characteristic expression: 'The painter, in order to obtain the most unaffected attitude, and the most poetic expression, engaged his sitter in a conversation concerning the sublime in art.' As a result, 'he caught from Blake's looks, as he related it, that rapt poetic expression which has rendered his portrait one of the finest of the English School'.[14] However, in Phillips's hands the topos of the moment of inspiration has become stereotyped and what is produced is, as David Piper puts it, 'an entirely competent but conventional formula of the poet as poet or artist . . .'[15]

Other portraits of Blake are primarily tributes of friendship. John Flaxman, who had known Blake since at least 1780, sketched him in 1804, in profile (Yale Center for British Art, Keynes pl. 5) and again full face (Fitzwilliam Museum, Keynes pl. 6). John Linnell, Blake's chief friend in his later years, showed him conversing with the artist John Varley (Fitzwilliam Museum, Keynes pl. 30), perhaps about the visionary heads he sometimes drew in Varley's presence. Linnell also drew Blake at a number of other moments—for instance, looking downwards meditatively so as to accentuate his wide forehead (Fitzwilliam Museum, Keynes pl. 24) wearing a wide-brimmed hat on Hampstead Heath (Fitzwilliam Museum, Keynes pl. 33). A drawing of Blake (Robert N. Essick Collection, Keynes pl. 35) looking directly at the viewer may also be by Linnell or very likely by Blake him-

[13] *Life and Posthumous Writings of William Cowper, Esq.* (Chichester, 1803), frontispiece to vol. i.

[14] G. E. Bentley, Jr., *Blake Records* (Oxford: Clarendon, 1969), 182–3, from Cunningham's *The Cabinet Gallery of Pictures* (London, 1833).

[15] Piper, *The Image of the Poet*, 113. The portrait is reproduced as pl. 121. All the portraits of Blake are reproduced by Sir Geoffrey Keynes in *The Complete Portraiture of William and Catherine Blake* (London: Trianon/William Blake Trust, 1977).

self.[16] George Richmond sketched the aged Blake (Fitzwilliam Museum, Keynes pl. 36) again wearing the wide-brimmed hat, walking resolutely forward with the aid of a stick. Blake's young friend Frederick Tatham drew a portrait head (Yale Center for British Art, Keynes pl. 41) from memory a few years after Blake's death and superimposed it against an idealized head of Blake imagined as young man, the latter based on a drawing that has been attributed to Catherine Blake.[17] Thanks to these flowers of friendship, we have ample evidence of how Blake appeared, especially in his later years, to a number of artists who knew him well. In addition, some literal details are supplied by the life-mask that Blake submitted to have taken by J. S. Deville, who was interested in his head for phrenological reasons, just as J. G. Spurzheim would be in Coleridge's. According to Blake's friend George Richmond, Deville 'wished to have a cast of Blake's head as representative of the imaginative faculty'.[18] Because taking the cast was a painful process, the result, as Richmond explained, looked far too severe for Blake, and that is also true of Spurzheim's mask of Coleridge.

Perhaps the contemporary poet whose portraiture parallels Coleridge's most closely during the years of their lives is, appropriately enough, William Wordsworth. Their stories start similarly with portraits by William Shuter and Robert Hancock;[19] both were the subjects of now unknown portraits by William Hazlitt, and both were drawn by Daniel Maclise. Twenty-three portraits of Wordsworth have been listed as executed before 1834, almost identical with the number portraits of Coleridge during his lifetime.[20] Of course since Wordsworth lived until 1850

[16] Robert Essick (personal communication) observes that the eyes resemble those in a number of Blake's drawings, such as *Adam Naming the Beasts* (Pollok House, Glasgow).

[17] See Keynes, *Complete Portraiture*, 118–20, 144, pls. 4, 41.

[18] See Bentley, *Blake Records*, 278.

[19] See Frances Blanshard, *Portraits of Wordsworth* (Ithaca, NY: Cornell University Press, 1959), 140–2 and pls. 1–2.

[20] See ibid. 140–60. The present study lists twenty-six Coleridge portraits (exclusive of replicas) known to have been executed during his lifetime; however, the images of Coleridge by Rippingille (Cat. no. 20) and by Mottram after Doyle (Cat. no. 19) were

and was a famous man during his late years, the number of his portraits greatly increased during that time. The changing popularity of these pictures, early and late, tells us almost as much about changes in public taste as it does about those in Wordsworth's appearance. If pride of place in the principal Wordsworth biographies is a reliable indication, the idealized images of the poet as the Sage of Rydal Mount painted by Henry William Pickersgill in 1832–3 (St John's College, Cambridge, Blanshard pl. 14*b*) and by Benjamin Robert Haydon in 1842 (NPG, Blanshard pl. 23) have given way to the sensitive beings depicted by Henry Edridge in 1806 (Wordsworth Museum, Grasmere, Blanshard pl. 3) and by Richard Carruthers in 1817 (Wordsworth Museum, Grasmere, Blanshard pl. 5). Edridge's drawing appears as the jacket illustration of Mary Moorman's *William Wordsworth: A Biography*,[21] as the frontispiece to volume i, and as the frontispiece of *William Wordsworth: A Life*[22] by Steven Gill, for which a detail of Carruthers's oil painting is the jacket illustration. (Carruthers also provides the cover design of Gill's anthology *William Wordsworth*[23] in the Oxford Authors series.) Casts of the life-mask (St John's College, Cambridge, and NPG, Blanshard pl. 4) taken by Haydon in 1815 are seldom reproduced, presumably because of their severity of expression—no doubt again the result of the subject's discomfort; while Haydon's 1818 drawing of the poet in an open-necked shirt (NPG, once popular in Wordsworth's circle as 'The Brigand'), has never gained much popularity outside of it, perhaps because of the difficulty of connecting it with the poet's characteristic subject-matter.

The same could not be said for the portraits of the most popular poet of the age. Lord Byron always seemed a creation of his

probably not from life. As Wordsworth appears in both these pictures and as they are not included by Blanshard, the overall comparison is not affected.

[21] Mary Moorman, *William Wordsworth: A Biography* (2 vols.; Oxford: Clarendon, 1957, 1965).

[22] S. Gill, *William Wordsworth: A Life* (Oxford: Clarendon, 1989).

[23] S. Gill, *William Wordsworth*, Oxford Authors, corr. edn. (Oxford and New York: Oxford University Press, 1990).

own imagination. This is seen at its most extreme in Thomas Phillips's portrait of Byron in Albanian dress (1813–14, version in the National Portrait Gallery). It has dash—Byron as his own Corsair—but no imaginative life; as Richard Brilliant remarks, 'There is nothing in this portrait of Byron to connect the passionate poet and adventurer with his own splendid achievements, or with the persona he was so actively creating at the time, except the token of exotic dress.'[24] Neither does Phillips's other well-known portrait of 1813–14, rendering its subject as darkly garbed, fair-skinned, and with classically beautiful features, go beyond the surface. Byron's own favourite was the delicate, large-eyed miniature he had painted for his friend Scrope Davies in 1815.[25] Other artists emphasized his melancholy, as did Richard Westall (1813, NPG); his dandyism, as did Count D'Orsay (1823); and his noble head, as did the sculptor Bertel Thorwaldsen (1817, Royal Collection).[26] With respect to the last, it is interesting that Byron refused the laurel wreath that had adorned the heads of some earlier poets. Byron knew a dead tradition when he met one, and he exercised remarkable control over his pictorial representation. He always sat for profile and three-quarter views so that the artist painted the left side of his face, and he rejected frontispieces that displeased him, demanding on two different occasions that his publisher, John Murray, destroy proofs and have plates broken.[27] In this respect, he resembled a later nineteenth-century poet, Walt Whitman, who carefully cultivated different images of himself and who vehemently objected to the portrait published with the first British edition of his poetry.[28]

[24] R. Brilliant, *Portraiture* (London: Reaktion Books, 1991), 101. The picture is reproduced by Piper, *The Image of the Poet*, fig. 142.

[25] Reproduced by Piper, *The Image of the Poet*, fig. 143.

[26] Ibid., figs. 144, 148, 151–2. D'Orsay's image is reproduced from a lithograph in the NPG.

[27] See Suzanne K. Hyman, 'Contemporary Portraits of Byron', in Charles E. Robinson (ed.), *Lord Byron and Some of his Contemporaries* (Newark: University of Delaware Press, 1982), 204–36.

[28] See Gay Wilson Allen, 'The Iconography of Walt Whitman', in Edward Haviland Miller (ed.), *The Artistic Legacy of Walt Whitman* (New York: New York University Press, 1970), 127–52; and Morton D. Paley, 'John Camden Hotten and the First British Editions of Walt Whitman—"A Nice Milky Cocoa-Nut" ', *Publishing History*, 6 (1979), 18–20.

When we turn from Byron, whose life was so rich in visual documentation, to his two younger contemporaries, the results are strikingly different. Shelley appears to have little interest in having his portrait taken. All that we have of him as an adult are some pencil sketches by his friend Edward Elleker Williams and a painting, unfinished at the time of the poet's death, by Amelia Curran.[29] The pencil sketches showing a delicate, rather ethereal young man are the ones most confidently ascribed to Williams. Much different is another attributed to him in which the sitter appears almost hulking, with staring blue eyes and black hair turning to grey at the sides.[30] It is hard to reconcile these very different images, especially as they would all have to have been drawn within an eighteen-month period. Amelia Curran began her Shelley portrait in Florence in 1819 but did not finish it until after Shelley's death, when she gave it to Mary Shelley. Wearing an open-necked shirt and holding a quill pen in his left hand, the poet gazes expressionlessly at the reader. It could be said, as it has been of Curran's portrait of Claire Clairmont, that 'it almost resembles a wooden doll'.[31] It is therefore understandable that later artists have tried to fill the need for a satisfactory representation of Shelley. Their attempts include sculptor Marianne Hunt's idealized bust (Eton College), wide-eyed and wild-haired, Onslow Ford's drowned hermaphrodite (University College, Oxford), and Tim Gados's sensitive-looking, pensive youth.[32] As if in ironic confirmation of the view that the deep truth is imageless, we have no truly satisfying portrait of Shelley.

[29] See Newman Ivey White, *Shelley* (New York: Knopf, 1940), app. V, 'The Portraits and Busts of Shelley', ii. 518–38. All the portraits of Shelley, including one of him as a boy aged 7 or 8 (Morgan Library), are reproduced by White.

[30] Reproduced by White as the frontispiece to *Shelley*, vol. i. White notes that this drawing bears the false signature of R[obert] Hancock.

[31] Robert Gittings and Jo Manton, *Claire Clairmont and the Shelleys* (Oxford and New York: Oxford University Press, 1992), 49. The Clairmont portrait (Newstead Abbey) is reproduced as the jacket illustration of this book.

[32] The Hunt bust appears on the jacket of James Rieger's *The Mutiny Within: The Heresies of Percy Bysshe Shelley* (New York: George Braziller, 1967); the Shelley Monument in *The Image of the Poet*, pls. 155, 156. Gados's picture, based on the known life portraits, is featured on the cover of *Shelley's Poetry and Prose*, ed. Donald H. Reiman and Sharon Powers (New York and London: W. W. Norton, 1977).

John Keats was far from indifferent to having his portrait taken, and in his case it was financial limitations that prevented him from presenting more images of himself to his friends and loved ones. He could not afford to buy for his sister Fanny the miniature (NPG) that his friend Joseph Severn exhibited at the Royal Academy in 1819, opting instead for a silhouette by another friend, Charles Armitage Brown (Keats Memorial House, Hampstead).[33] Severn's portrait shows the poet in a conventional meditative pose, chin resting on his left hand and arm. His right hand lies on a manuscript, and his right eye exhibits the gleam that we have seen in the eyes of some previous poets. Severn's more informal drawings carry more conviction: an animated profile (1816, V. & A.) and a head of Keats, hair dishevelled and eyes closed, dying in Rome (1821, Keats-Shelley Memorial House, Rome).[34] The profile drawing that Brown made in 1819 (NPG) has a sense of presence, even though the fist that supports the subject's head is too large for the rest.[35] Benjamin Robert Haydon sketched Keats as an intently gazing spectator for his painting *Christ's Entry into Jerusalem*, and he also took a life-mask which, unlike the masks of Blake, Wordsworth, and Coleridge, has a beautifully serene expression.[36] Keats gave casts of this mask to friends, humorously remarking to Charles Cowden Clarke: 'You may now look at Minerva's Ægis with impunity, seeing that my awful Visage did not turn you into a John Doree you have accordingly a legitimate title to a Copy—[.]'[37] After Keats's death in Rome, a mask was taken, possibly by the sculptor

[33] See Keats's letter to Fanny Keats, 17 June 1819, *The Letters of John Keats*, ed. Hyder E. Rollins (Cambridge, Mass.: Harvard University Press, 1958). The miniature and silhouette are reproduced in Walter Jackson Bate, *John Keats* (Cambridge, Mass.: Harvard University Press, 1963), figs. 9, 8. The reader is warned to use with great care the unreliable *Portraits of Keats* by Donald Parson (Cleveland and New York: World, 1954). There is, for example, no portrait of Keats by William Blake!

[34] Reproduced in Aileen Ward, *John Keats: The Making of a Poet* (New York: Viking, 1963), figs. 8, 14.

[35] Reproduced ibid., fig. 9.

[36] The sketch (1816, NPG), is reproduced in Piper, *The Image of the Poet*, fig. 129. The life-mask (Keats Memorial House, Hampstead) is reproduced as the frontispiece to Ward's *John Keats*.

[37] *Letters*, ed. Rollins, 17 Dec. 1817, i. 121. A 'John Doree' (John Dory) is a fish.

Canova's mask-maker, Gherardi,[38] and Joseph Severn used both the mask and a cast of Keats's hand in painting Keats reading under the picture of his Presider at Wentworth Place (NPG).[39] Wooden and sentimental, this representation both reflects and contributes to the sentimentalization of Keats that took place after his death.

This conspectus helps us relate Coleridge portraiture to that of the other major Romantic poets. Unlike Shelley, Coleridge was painted and drawn by a variety of artists; unlike Blake (with one exception) and Keats, who depended for their portraits almost entirely upon their circle of artistic friends, Coleridge had some commissioned portraits taken, though he himself was seldom the one who paid for them. Neither an object of collective fantasy like Byron (who could also well afford to pay for his portraits) nor a national institution as Wordsworth was becoming during Coleridge's later years, Coleridge still attracted a number of artists eager to sketch or paint him and a number of sponsors wishing to pay for portraits. Coleridge was more than passively co-operative in these enterprises: he took trouble with his sittings, travelling, though in increasingly bad health, to artist's studios and giving advice as to how he thought he should be shown. As a result, we have a significant body of portraits of Coleridge. We now turn to these, and to what they tell us.

[38] See Robert Gittings, *The Mask of Keats* (Cambridge, Mass.: Harvard University Press, 1966), 1–4. The original has disappeared. Gittings reproduces as his frontispiece a cast from a private collection; another cast is at the Keats Memorial House, Hampstead.

[39] Reproduced in Piper, *The Image of the Poet*, fig. 129.

2

The Life Portraits of Coleridge

SAMUEL TAYLOR COLERIDGE did not like his own face. Here is his description of it to John Thelwall, written on 19 November 1796:

As to me, my face, unless when animated by immediate eloquence, expresses great Sloth, & great, indeed almost ideotic good nature. 'Tis a mere carcase of a face: fat, flabby, & expressive chiefly of inexpression.—Yet, I am told, that my eyes, eyebrows, & forehead are physiognomically good—; but as to this the Deponent knoweth not . . . I cannot breathe thro' my nose—so my mouth, with its sensual thick lips, is almost always open.[1]

Yet a description by Dorothy Wordsworth written in the following year, while incorporating some of the same details, has a much different emphasis:

At first I thought him very plain [she wrote], that is, for about three minutes: he is pale and thin, has a wide mouth, thick lips, and not very good teeth, longish loose-growing half-curling rough black hair. But if you hear him speak for five minutes you think no more of them. His eye is large and full, not dark but grey; such an eye as would receive from a heavy soul the dullest expression; but it speaks every emotion of his animated mind; it has more of the 'poet's eye in a fine frenzy rolling' than I ever witnessed. He has fine dark eye-brows, and an overhanging forehead.[2]

Coleridge's curly hair, a prominent feature of two of the early portraits, glowed in the memory of a Bristol lady who met the

[1] *CL* i. 259–60.

[2] *EY* 189. Conjecturally dated June 1797 and as written to Mary Hutchinson. It's interesting that, after reading this description many years later, Coleridge's daughter Sara noted, 'I thought my father had been rather fleshy always . . .', *Sara Coleridge and Henry Reed*, ed. Nathan Leslie Broughton (Ithaca, NY: Cornell University Press, 1937), 98.

poet in 1796 and later described his appearance to Thomas De Quincey, emphasizing 'his beautiful black hair, which lay in masses of natural curls half-way down his back'.[3] In these descriptions we find some details that recur in any discussion of Coleridge portraiture. His hair was rich and beautiful, and the upper part of the head and face was noble; the lower, especially the lips and teeth, could appear gross; but when his features were animated in conversation or in reading poetry, all disagreeables evaporated. Beginning with the earliest portraits, the difference between the static and dynamic aspects of Coleridge's face, as well as between the upper and lower parts of it, was the subject at various times of comments by the poet, his friends, and the artists themselves.

The 1790s

The first three portraits of Coleridge are associated with his Bristol area friends Joseph Cottle and Thomas Poole. They belong to the period of the latter 1790s, a period of unusually intense activity when Coleridge was actively pursuing projects in poetry (especially the ambitious 'Religious Musings'), theology (including the *Lectures on Revealed Religion*), journalism (*The Watchman*), and politics. These were also the years of Coleridge's close friendship with Robert Southey, his engagement and marriage to Sara Fricker, and the never-to-be-realized plan for a Utopian community on the banks of the Susquehanna. Painted by lesser-known but nevertheless highly professional artists, all three portraits have in common the imaging of the poet as a young man of heightened sensibility and advanced intellect.

Two of these pictures were commissioned by Coleridge's friend and Bristol publisher Joseph Cottle, who in the later 1790s assembled a portrait gallery of his literary friends, including

[3] Postscript to 'Coleridge and Opium Eating', *The Collected Writings of Thomas De Quincey*, ed. David Masson (Edinburgh: Adam & Charles Black, 1890), v. 212–14).

1. Peter Vandyke

Southey, Lamb, Wordsworth, and Amos Cottle. For the first known Coleridge portrait (Cat no. 1), executed in 1795, Cottle chose Peter Vandyke (1729–99), who claimed descent from the great portraitist Anthony Van Dyck.[4] Invited from Holland by Reynolds to assist him with the drapery of portraits, Vandyke had shown his own work in London during the period 1762–72—seventeen pictures at the Free Society of Artists and two at the Society of Artists.[5] Among his other works was a striking full-length portrait of a tennis player.[6] He was evidently professionally recognized but not successful enough to be associated with the Royal Academy or to show pictures in its annual exhibitions, and in 1771 the Free Society of Artists voted him ten guineas in relief of distress.[7] He later settled in Bristol, perhaps in order to escape the highly competitive atmosphere of London. In his depiction of Coleridge (NPG, no. 192), his subject is portrayed as an icon of the Man of Feeling—lips moist, hazel eyes glistening, natural shoulder-length hair falling in dark auburn, somewhat disordered ringlets. The mouth is slightly open, showing some upper front teeth, but Vandyke attempted to solve the problem of the lips by arranging them in a Cupid's bow. Cottle himself vouches for the verisimilitude of this image ('a better likeness was never taken') and remarks that 'it has the additional advantage of exhibiting Mr C. in one of his animated conversations, the expression of which the painter has in a good degree preserved.'[8] This theme of animation—its presence or absence—was to become an important one in the discussion of Coleridge portraits by his friends and other contemporaries. Yet, despite Cottle's statement, the sitter's expression appears more dreamy

[4] A. Cottle, *Early Recollections* (London, 1837), p. xxxvi.

[5] *Dict.* 285.

[6] Ellis Waterhouse notes that this picture, signed and dated 1779, shows the influence of Zoffany and could perhaps represent an actor playing a role. See *The Dictionary of British Eighteenth Century Painters in Oils and Crayons* (Woodbridge: Antique Collectors' Club, 1981), 345.

[7] See William T. Whitley, *Artists and their Friends in England 1700–1799* (2 vols.; London and Boston: The Medici Society, 1928), i. 190. According to Whitley, Vandyke also assisted Allan Ramsay.

[8] Cottle, *Early Recollections*, p. xxxi.

than conversational. When the image was reproduced in R. Woodman's engraved frontispiece for Cottle's book, it became tamer: the parted lips were almost closed, the flamboyant cravat reduced in size, and the sense of the poet's face virtually gleaming out of the background was lost.

The Vandyke portrait struck E. H. Coleridge as remarkably like an engraving after a portrait of Coleridge's contemporary the German poet Novalis.[9] There can be no question of direct influence here, as the engraving was not executed until 1845,[10] but the portrait of Novalis by Franz Gareis does follow the archetype of Sensibility also rendered in Vandyke's image of the poet. In E. H. Coleridge's instance a mere comparison was intended, but sometimes similarities of age and of costume, along with the conventions of the half-length portrait can lead to some confusion, as appears to have occurred in the case of a portrait that has been attributed to John Opie and conjectured to be of Coleridge.[11] Whether this painting is by Opie or not, the sitter bears only a generic resemblance to the subject of the Vandyke portrait and any relationship to Coleridge is highly doubtful.

In 1796 a second portrait of Coleridge (Cat. no. 2) was executed for Joseph Cottle by Robert Hancock (1730–1817), who also produced a drawing of Southey for Cottle in that year and portraits of Lamb and Wordsworth in 1798 (all four are now in the NPG collection). Hancock was best known as a creator of prints for porcelain, which involved transferring a design printed in adhesive pigments on thin tissue paper to the porcelain ware.[12] Considered one of the best practitioners in his field, he had produced well-known images, in jet enamel, of Frederick the Great,

[9] MS Notes on Coleridge portraits, MS 79. 360, the Harry Ransom Center for the Humanities, University of Texas. Further references to this document will be to MS Notes.

[10] I am indebted to Detlef W. Dörrbecker of the University of Trier for information about the Novalis portrait. The original, attributed to Franz Gareis, is in the Weissenfels Museum. It has been conjecturally dated 1799 or 1801.

[11] See Anon., 'Coleridge by Opie?', *Country Life*, 154 (1973), 1537.

[12] Cyril Cook, 'A Pioneer in Porcelain Decoration', *Country Life*, 26 (Jan. 1951), 250–1; see also Frances Blanshard, *Portraits of Wordsworth* (London: George Allen & Unwin, 1959), 42–3, 141; Joseph Burke, *English Art 1714–1800* (Oxford: Clarendon, 1976), 149.

2. Robert Hancock

General Wolfe, George II, and the Marquis of Granby, among others. He also engraved after contemporary British artists, most notably the figures of Comedy and Tragedy from Reynolds's *Garrick Between Tragedy and Comedy*. At the time that he painted Coleridge, Hancock appears no longer to have been active in porcelain decoration, but the small size of this portrait ($7 \times 5\frac{1}{8}$ in., compared to the Vandyke's 22×18 in.) may reflect the scale on which he was used to working. In this delicate rendering, the subject, says Cottle, is 'wearing precisely the garments that which Mr Coleridge wore when he preached his first sermon, in Mr Jardine's chapel, at Bath'.[13] Cottle also tells us that this picture 'has an additional interest from having been drawn when Mr C's spirits were in a state of depression on account of the failure of his "Watchman" ', and indeed in the *Biographia Literaria* Coleridge links this particular costume with *The Watchman* when he describes himself trying to sell subscriptions in his tour to the North, 'preaching by the way in most of the great towns, as an hireless volunteer, in a blue coat and white waistcoat, that not a rag of the Woman of Babylon might be seen on me'.[14] There is something poignant about this large-eyed image, and the characteristic parting of the lips may here be seen as conveying a breathless quality. Hancock's Coleridge is considerably thinner than Vandyke's. Perhaps the change in his weight can be linked to worries over *The Watchman*, as Cottle would have us believe, but, as we have seen, Dorothy Wordsworth described Coleridge as 'thin' in 1797; and De Quincey wrote that 'whereas, throughout his thirty-five years of opium he was rather corpulent . . . in 1796, when he had nearly accomplished his twenty-sixth year, he was slender in the degree most approved by ladies'.[15] Although

[13] Cottle, *Early Recollections*, i. p. xxxi; cf. i. 179: 'Mr. C. wore his blue coat and white waistcoat . . . He refused to wear a sable gown.'

[14] *BL* i. 179; cf. Cottle, *Early Recollections*, i. 179.

[15] De Quincey, Postscript, *Collected Writings*, v. 212–14. Presumably De Quincey, who did not meet Coleridge until 1807, is relying on the anonymous Bristol lady whose admiration of Coleridge's hair he had previously quoted. Yet Hazlitt remembered the Coleridge of 1798 as 'in his person . . . rather inclining to the corpulent, or like Lord Hamlet's 'somewhat fat and pursy'.—'My First Acquaintance with Poets', *The Complete Works*

the viewer would not know, unless cued by Cottle, that the sitter was a preacher, he or she would see in him an air of eager expectation, which is also transmitted by Woodman's engraving for the frontispiece of vol. ii of Cottle's *Early Recollections*.

Two other portraits of Coleridge were painted before the end of the eighteenth century. The first of these (Cat. no. 3) is associated with the poet's other close friend in the Bristol area, Thomas Poole, tanner and radical. The artist was identified by E. L. Griggs in 1956 as W. Shuter.[16] This may have been the William Shuter who exhibited thirty pictures of flowers and fruit at the Royal Academy, the Free Society of Artists, and the Society of Artists in London from 1774 to 1791.[17] In that case, we have another artist who, like Peter Vandyke, achieved a modest success in the metropolis and then migrated to the West Country. Shuter, then living at Nether Stowey, also painted a sensitive rendering of Poole in 1797 (in the collection of Judge King, Nether Stowey),[18] as well as a splendid half-length of Wordsworth (Cornell Wordsworth collection) for Cottle in the year that *Lyrical Ballads* was published.[19] He has also been identified as the painter of what Waterhouse terms 'an extremely provincial "Family group," signed and dated 1798.' His portrait of Coleridge, now

of William Hazlitt, ed. P. P. Howe (London and Toronto: J. M. Dent, 1933), xvii. 109. It may be that the young Coleridge's weight varied dramatically within comparatively short periods, as Byron's did (or as Byron thought it did).

[16] *CL* i, List of Illustrations. This is the first appearance of Shuter's name in connection with this portrait. No signature can be seen in the rather dark reproduction, and the location of the original is unknown. However, no signature is visible in the much clearer reproduction of Shuter's Wordsworth portrait in Blanshard's *Portraits of Wordsworth*, pl. 1, and the original is indeed signed in brown on a darker brown background in the lower right-hand corner: 'W. Shuter 1798' (I am grateful to Sarah McKibben for this information).

[17] *Royal Academy*, vii. 120, and *Dict.* 254. Alternatively, Ellis Waterhouse speculates that the portraitist may have been the son of the artist who showed landscapes and flower paintings from 1771 to 1779. See *Dictionary of British Eighteenth Century Painters*, 345.

[18] Reproduced in Elizabeth Sandford, *Thomas Poole and His Friends* (Over Stowey: Friarn, 1996), facing p. 20.

[19] The painter is identified by Cottle merely as 'an artist then at Stowey' (*Early Recollections*, i. 317 n.). See also Blanshard, *Portraits of Wordsworth*, 41–2, 140, and pl. 1; J. Wordsworth, M. C. Jaye, and R. Woof, *William Wordsworth and the Age of English Romanticism* (New Brunswick and London: Rutgers University Press, 1987), 211. This portrait of Wordsworth is the earliest known.

3. William Shuter

unfortunately untraced, may have been painted as a pendant to the Wordsworth portrait in 1798, but it did not belong to Cottle, as the list of portraits owned by him in *Early Recollections* shows. As it once belonged to Thomas Poole's collateral descendant Miss A. A. King of Newark Park, Oglesworth, Wotton-under-Edge,[20] it seems reasonable to assume that the original owner was Poole himself. The portrait depicts an alert-looking young man, wearing jacket and cravat as in the two previous depictions. Again, his mouth is slightly open, and in a copy once owned by E. L. Griggs[21] three upper teeth are visible. The original[22] showed the sitter holding a book in a position in which a minister might be depicted with the Bible. However, the lettering on the book cover reads 'HARTLEY,' an indication of the importance of Hartley's philosophy to Coleridge at a time when he could name his son 'David Hartley Coleridge, in honor of the great Master of Christian Philosophy'.[23] During this period, Coleridge thought he could synthesize associationism, necessitarianism, and millennialism, elements of which he found in Hartley's writings, in a unified philosophy that would explain human existence and be compatible with Unitarianism. The smartly dressed, large-eyed young man who looks out at us from Shuter's portrait seems to be underlining 'HARTLEY' with his right index finger, pointing the way.

As Shuter's original portrait is untraced, it is known only through engravings, photographs, and copies. At least three of the latter were painted, for James and Anne Gillman, Henry Nelson Coleridge, and Joseph Henry Green, in 1835–6. Two copies are currently known, both trimmed down.[24] One, show-

[20] See *RP* i. 120.

[21] Humanities Research Center, Austin, 78. 321. 2. As the book is included, this photo with an oil overlay is presumably based on the original. Verso stamped 'S. Crowden Clement A.R.P.S./The Studio/Church Street/Wotton-Under-Edge, Glos.' The dimensions are given as $8\frac{1}{8} \times 5\frac{5}{16}$ in. (20.6 × 13.5 cm.), but were these the dimensions of the original as well?

[22] See reproduction in *CL* i, frontispiece.

[23] Letter to Benjamin Flower, 2 Nov. 1796, *CL* i. 247.

[24] In HNC's correspondence in the BL there are letters to Thomas Poole arranging to have a portrait owned by Poole copied. On 5 Sept. 1835 HNC asked for permission 'to have a copy or copies taken of the admirable picture left with me by Mr. Stutfield', on

ing the subject with chestnut-reddish hair, is at the Highgate Literary and Scientific Institution. Another, showing Coleridge with auburn hair, was sold at Sotheby's in December 1995 and acquired by the Friends of Coleridge for Coleridge Cottage.[25] As neither of these copies includes the important detail of the book held by Coleridge in the original, it is possible that the latter was trimmed down before the copies were made.[26] On Derwent Coleridge's initiative, a copy of the Shuter portrait made by Samuel Laurence, a portrait artist in his own right,[27] and owned by Sara Coleridge, was selected for reproduction as the frontispiece of the *Poetical Works* of 1852. Sara Coleridge took strong exception to the fidelity of this image of her father. In her Preface to the edition she wrote:

The Portrait has been engraved from a picture of S. T. Coleridge, at twenty-six years of age, which originally belonged to the poet's

behalf of Joseph Henry Green and James and Anne Gillman as well as himself ('Mr. Stutfield' was Charles Stutfield, Jun., of Hackney, who had been tutored in logic by Coleridge; see *CL* v. 31, 204). On 21 Sept. HNC wrote to Poole, thanking him for giving permission; and on 16 Apr. 1836 he confirmed that the three copies had been made and asked how to send the original back, a request repeated on 31 May. (BL, Add. MS 35344, fos. 120, 122^v, 127, 129). EHC noted in his MS that copies were made for James Gillman, Henry Nelson Coleridge, and Joseph Henry Green, and that the latter's passed on through Green's nieces to Derwent Coleridge and then to himself. (As the borrowed portrait is not described or otherwise characterized, it could in theory have been either Shuter's or the 'German portrait' (on which see below); however, as Poole did not really like the German portrait and may even have parted with it by 1835, it is less likely to have been the one copied.)

[25] 'English School, oil on panel, head and shoulders, in dark coat and wearing a white cravat, *c.11 × 9 inches, cleaned, in gilt frame [nineteenth century]*': Sotheby's catalogue, *English Literature and History*, sale no. LN5449, lot 145. See *Coleridge Bulletin*, NS 7 (Spring 1996), 64.

[26] According to Professor J. C. C. Mays (private communication), the tenant of Newark Park reported in 1984 that when he had last seen the portrait it had been cut down to fit over a fireplace in a smaller room in the cottage of a Mr Cartwright, nephew to Miss King, in Beaminster. According to Professor Mays's informant, Mr Cartwright died in 1975 and Mrs Cartwright in 1976, after which the estate was inherited by Mr Cartwright's niece in Australia.

[27] Laurence also did portraits of DC and of SC. The former was the basis of a lithograph by J. H. Lynch, dated 15 Nov. 1850. That of SC, which in Edith Coleridge's opinion contained 'a good deal of likeness' (Carl L. Grantz, 'Letters of Sara Coleridge: Calendar and Index to her Manuscript Correspondence', Ph.D. Diss., Austin, Tex., 1968, no. 98, i. 68), is reproduced as the frontispiece to Bradford Mudge's *Sara Coleridge: A Victorian Daughter* (London and New Haven: Yale University Press, 1989). Among Laurence's other original portraits is a striking one of Tennyson of *c.*1840 (see Piper, *The Image of the Poet*, 166 and fig. 181).

admirable friend, Thomas Poole, of Nether Stowey, by the kind permission of R. P. King, Esq., of Brislington, near Bath, its present owner. It is presented not as altogether satisfactory, but as the best and most interesting record of the Poet's youthful face that was to be obtained.[28]

Her actual feelings, as expressed in a portion of the Preface that remained in manuscript, were more vehement.

It is difficult indeed to conceive, that the countenance of him who wrote 'The Ancient Mariner' and 'Kubla Khan' displayed so little of fire and energy as appears in this representation; or that the lover of long pedestrian excursions and mountain rambles, with health as yet unbroken, was so wanting in the outward air of vigour . . . This portrait, while it brings into prominence the 'wide mouth' and 'heavy low hung lip,' flat nose and pale cheek of the youthful Coleridge—(that languor and pallor were not at any period, of life *habitual* to his appearance we know by the testimony of many witnesses) is far from doing even such measure of justice as might have been done to the poet's countenance.[29]

In fact, using an engraving after the Shuter portrait as the frontispiece was entirely Derwent's idea, as Sara makes clear in a letter to her brother dated 22 January 1852.[30] As far as her own view was concerned, she wrote to Derwent on February 22, 'I can hardly bear to let *that* face be stamped upon the youthful STC without any kind of protest'.[31] Sara Coleridge's condemnation evidently applied to Laurence's copy as well as to the engraving; and there is no reason to imagine that she would have liked the original any better. Remarking to her brother on Laurence's liking for the 'Poole portrait', as she called it, Sara wrote: 'He was the copiest of it. But thou knowest he likes what is ugly and despises what is pretty.'[32] Although in Moxon's editions of the

[28] *The Complete Poetical Works of Samuel Taylor Coleridge*, ed. D. and S. Coleridge (London: Moxon, 1852), p. xiv.

[29] Grantz, no. 111, i. 72.

[30] Grantz, no. 95, i. 66.

[31] Grantz, no. 111, i. 72.

[32] MS in HRC, Grantz, no. 95, i. 66. However, Sara was not always negative about Samuel Laurence. In a letter to Henry Reed dated 3 July 1850, she characterized Laurence as 'A very accomplished and intelligent artist of my acquaintance' (S. Coleridge, *Sara Coleridge and Henry Reed*, ed. L. N. Broughton (Ithaca, NY: Cornell University Press, 1937), 49).

II. An unknown artist in Germany, replica

Complete Poetical Works, W. Holl's lithograph after Shuter was retained through 1863, in 1870 a fine, unsigned stipple engraving after Allston's 1814 portrait was substituted as a frontispiece. Sara, who had died in 1852, would have been pleased, for that was her favourite portrayal of Coleridge (see below). Nevertheless, we must remember that Shuter's original was probably painted in 1798, while Coleridge's daughter was born in late December 1802 and her father left on the first stage of his trip to Malta just a year later. As her remarks indicate, her judgement is based not on any recollection of her father's appearance when young but on an idea of what the poet 'who wrote "The Ancient Mariner" and "Kubla Khan" ' *ought* to have looked like. To her, as to many others, the *gravitas* of Allston's somewhat idealized depiction suited this idea better than a toothy, round-faced young man pointing to a volume of Hartley.

The last Coleridge portrait of the eighteenth century (Cat. no. 4) was executed while the poet was in Germany in 1798–9. The identity of the artist and the circumstances of its execution are unknown, which is all the more frustrating because it is by far the most exciting image of the young Coleridge. E. H. Coleridge remarked that here Coleridge 'figured as the creature & apostle of Romance', and imagined the poet as looking like this as he recited *Christabel* on his journey through the Hartz Mountains.[33] Some features of this portrait correspond to William Hazlitt's recollection of Coleridge as he appeared in 1798—'His forehead was broad and high, light as if built of ivory, with large projecting eyebrows, and his eyes rolling beneath them like a sea with darkened lustre . . . His hair . . . was then black and glossy as the raven's, and fell in smooth masses over his forehead.'[34] Even more than Vandyke's portrayal, this picture belongs to the

[33] EHC, MS Notes.

[34] Hazlitt, 'My First Acquaintance with Poets', *Complete Works*, xxvii. 109. In part of the passage I have omitted, Hazlitt also remarks 'his nose, the rudder of the face, the index of the will, was small, feeble, nothing—like what he has done'. Yet this accords neither with other contemporary descriptions nor with portraits of Coleridge during this period. Among all the Coleridge portraits, the poet's nose is small only in that by Moses Haughton and the copy after it (see below).

prototype also to be followed by Franz Gareis in his depiction of Novalis in 1801. Here we see the poet as the fully fledged Romantic *schöne Seele*, an exalted being at the same time spiritualized and erotic, exuding a sense of androgynous beauty. It may have been something about the sense of vulnerability in this image that caused Coleridge to remark, 'I have never to the best of my recollection felt the fear of Death but once—that was, yesterday when I delivered the picture . . .'[35]

The portrait was presented by the poet to his patron Josiah Wedgwood and sent from Göttingen with Anthony Hamilton, one of Coleridge's German circle.[36] Although it may be assumed to have reached Wedgwood, as the accompanying letter is in the Wedgwood Museum, its present location is unknown. At least one copy was produced for Coleridge and sent by him to Thomas Poole in 1802; on 7 March the poet wrote, 'I am glad you have received the German picture'.[37] However, Poole, who evidently thought of Coleridge as a seeker of the natural sublime, did not find his idea of the poet in it. On 2 May 1802 he wrote:

> I have at last received your *German picture*. It is a good picture—certainly like you—but it *wants character*. Nevertheless, I value it much. It is a very agreeable picture, and it gives one pleasure to look at; but it is *Mr. Coleridge* and not *Coleridge*. You are in the drawing-room, and not in the vales of Quantock, or on the top of Skiddaw.[38]

Such a response from a close friend who took a lively interest in Coleridge portraiture reminds us how a representation of the poet intended for one viewer (in this instance Wedgwood) could be jarring for another. Poole either gave or willed this picture to his sometime apprentice and later business partner Thomas Ward, towards whom the bachelor Poole felt almost as a father.[39]

[35] *CL* i. 517, letter to Josiah Wedgwood dated 21 May 1799.

[36] Ibid.; see Richard Holmes, *Coleridge: Early Visions* (London: Hodder & Stoughton, 1989), 235.

[37] *CL* ii. 800.

[38] M. E. Sandford, *Thomas Poole and His Friends* (London and New York: Macmillan, 1888), ii. 79.

[39] See Wensley Pithey, 'A German Coleridge Portrait', *TLS* (1935), 76; Walter H. Cam, 'A Coleridge Portrait', Ibid. 92; Griggs, *CL* i. 230 n.; *RP* i. 120. According to Cam,

Referred to by Coleridge as 'that young man with the soul-beaming face' in a letter to Poole,[40] Ward transcribed many of Coleridge's letters to Poole, especially those from Germany. On one occasion he sent Coleridge some quill pens, and Coleridge addressed at least two letters to him from Germany.[41] The copy is reported to bear on the back of its frame the following information as to its provenance:

> Portrait of Coleridge 1798–9
> taken in Germany
> and given by the Poet
> to Thomas Ward
> This memorandum
> was written by the
> youngest daughter
> of the above.
>
> Kate Ward
>
> Signed and confirmed by his
> other daughters
>
> Mary Isabella Ward
> Agnes Scott
> 1st January 1907.[42]

Although the inscription has it that the picture was given directly to Ward, it would be understandable that after so long a lapse of time Ward's daughters could have been mistaken about this, not realizing that Poole had owned it first.

The first four Coleridge portraits were painted by artists who were highly competent but not famous. Coleridge himself may

who inherited the picture from his great-aunt Kate Ward, the picture was given by Poole to Ward. Among these sources, only Walker notes that this portrait is a copy, and so it is important to emphasize that the original, presented by Coleridge to Wedgwood, is unlocated.

[40] *CL* i. 230. [41] 7 and 8 Oct. 1799, *CL* i. 536–8.

[42] This information about provenance comes from a letter by Richard Tolson in a memorandum dated 1 May 1988 in the Archive of HLSI. According to this memorandum, on the death of Kate Ward in 1925 the picture passed to her great-nephew, Dr Walter Holcroft Cam (d. 8 Dec. 1937) and was later inherited by Thomas Ward's great-granddaughter, Mrs Valdez Gardner.

have paid only for the two versions of the German portrait, although even that is not certain. All were executed for friends of the poet. Different aspects of his identity are emphasized, presumably those qualities that the intended owner valued (we see how this could misfire when a portrait intended for Wedgwood was copied and given to Poole), but all show aspects of a young man at the cutting edge of the 1790s—poetic sensibility, intellectual awareness, and poignant physical attractiveness. After Coleridge returned to England in 1799, this image of the poet gradually changed, culminating in James Northcote's rendering of his subject in 1804 as an icon of high Romanticism.

1802–1804

As early as 1801 Coleridge was thinking of going abroad for his health, and the portraits executed between his return from Germany and his departure for Malta were meant to appeal to 'the ideal sense of the friend not present' during what would be a more protracted absence. The first of these (Cat. no. 5), painted by the miniaturist John Hazlitt, was shown at the Royal Academy in 1802 (no. 839) and puffed in the *Courier*, where Coleridge had influence. The poet wrote to Thomas Poole on 7 May: 'There is one [picture] (I see by the Newspapers) in the Exhibition of me/ what it is, or whose, I do not know, but I guess it must be the miniature, which Hazlitt promised to Mrs Coleridge; but he did not give it to her, because I never finished my sittings.'[43] There followed the familiar lament over his own features: 'Mine is not a *picturesque* Face/Southey's was made for a picture.' Unfortunately, this portrait is at present untraced, and our only clue as to what it was like is a description of it in the 1920 sale catalogue of the celebrated Francis Wellesley collection:

[43] *CL* ii. 800.

425. John Hazlitt 1767–1837

SAMUEL TAYLOR COLERIDGE. Almost half-length, viewed to the left. He wears a green coat and white waistcoat spotted with blue, white neck-cloth, brown hair falling to the shoulders.

water-colour *Oval, $4\frac{1}{4} \times 5$ in. On paper.*[44]

Coleridge's pose and costume, then, was something like those in the Vandyke and the German portraits, but this picture was a miniature executed in watercolour. As the buyer in 1920, according to annotated copies of this catalogue in the British Museum Department of Prints and Drawings and in the British Library, was 'Wordsworth',[45] it can be hoped that the picture will one day be traced.

This portrait has sometimes been reassigned to John's younger brother William Hazlitt,[46] but no evidence supports this. John Hazlitt was a highly professional artist, as can be seen by his fine portrait of Joseph Lancaster in the National Portrait Gallery. John exhibited seventy-three pictures at the Royal Academy from 1788 to 1819,[47] while William exhibited there only twice (1802 and 1805). That Coleridge knew John is indicated by a Notebook entry conjecturally dated 18 January 1800. 'Hazlitt, the painter, told me that a picture never looks so well as when the Pallet was by the side of it—/Association with the glow of Production.'[48] It is unlikely that in his own notebook Coleridge would refer to William Hazlitt, whom he had known since 1798, as 'Hazlitt, the painter', while it would be entirely reasonable for him to distinguish John from William by this epithet. (In her note to this entry,

[44] Sotheby, Wilkinson, and Hodge, *Catalogue of the Well-Known and Valuable Collection of Plumbago, Pen and Ink, and Coloured Pencil Drawings and Miniatures*, 18 June 1920, p. 11. On the importance of the miniatures in the Wellesley collection, see Dr G. C. Williamson, 'Mr. Francis Wellesley's Collection of Miniatures and Drawings', pt. 1, *The Connoisseur*, 60 (June 1918), 63–75.

[45] Presumably Gordon Graham Wordsworth, who purchased at this sale a John Hazlitt portrait supposed to be of William Wordsworth (now in the Wordsworth Museum, Grasmere). The Coleridge portrait sold for £4, the Wordsworth for £14.

[46] See Crawford, 650. [47] *Royal Academy*, iv. 52–3.

[48] *CN* i. 632 (for dating see i. 500). Coleridge could have met John Hazlitt through mutual political friends such as John Thelwall and William Godwin. See W. Carew Hazlitt, *Four Generations of a Literary Family* (4 vols.; London: George Redway, 1897), i. 88.

Kathleen Coburn identifies 'the Painter' as John.) The list of exhibitors in the Royal Academy exhibition catalogue contributes to the confusion with a misprint, identifying the painter of the Coleridge portrait (no. 839) and three others[49] as 'T. Hazlitt', but there are several reasons for considering 'T' as a misprint for 'J'. In this same catalogue, 'W. Hazlitt' is represented by one picture—'688 Portrait of his father'—while J. Hazlitt is not represented at all. Yet John Hazlitt exhibited every year from 1788 to 1801 and again in 1803, 1804, and 1805. As W. Hazlitt was included in the 1802 catalogue and J. Hazlitt was not, it seems very likely that the printer mistook a *J* for a *T*, creating 'T. Hazlitt', whose name never again appears in a Royal Academy catalogue. William's grandson W. Carew Hazlitt assigned the Coleridge miniature to John Hazlitt, and this has been followed by more recent biographers.[50] There is no reason to reattribute this portrait to William.

William Hazlitt did paint Coleridge in the following year. The difference between William's artistic aims and John's have been aptly characterized by W. Carew Hazlitt: 'John Hazlitt rapidly attained the height of his fame and the limit of his faculty. His miniatures, by which it is fairest to estimate him, were admirable in mechanical execution, in colour, and in drapery; but it was a widely different sort and degree of success to which his brother aspired and despaired of ever reaching.'[51] William had begun studying painting in London in the autumn of 1798,[52] and in 1802 he exhibited a portrait of his father at the Royal Academy.[53] He took advantage of the Peace of Amiens that year to travel to Paris and copy master paintings in the Louvre. After returning to London in February 1803, he began what he hoped would be a pro-

[49] The others were: 712, Portrait of Mrs Hazlitt; 753 Portrait of Mrs Carsburgh; and 826 Portraits of Mrs Favell, Mr J. Robinson, and Mrs N. Robinson. The last could have been a group portrait or, more likely, three portraits under a single entry.

[50] W. Carew Hazlitt, *Memoirs of William Hazlitt* (2 vols.; London, 1867), i. 82–3; P. P. Howe, *Life of William Hazlitt* (Harmondsworth: Penguin, 1949 (1947)), 89; Catherine Macdonald Maclean, *Born Under Saturn: A Biography of William Hazlitt* (London: Collins, 1943), 126.

[51] *Four Generations of a Literary Family*, i. 88.

[52] See Carl Woodring in *TT* i. 198 n. 33.

[53] No. 688. In 1805 he would exhibit 'a gentleman' (no. 585).

fessional career as a portrait artist. His Coleridge portrait, perhaps preceded by a sketch (Cat. nos. 6 and 7), was begun when Hazlitt visited the Lakes in July 1803,[54] and on 23 July Coleridge wrote to Wordsworth, 'Every single person without one exception cries out!—What a likeness!—but the face is too long! You have a round face! Hazlitt knows this, but he will not alter it. Why?—because the Likeness with him is a secondary Consideration—he wants it to be a fine picture'.[55] On 1 August Coleridge wrote enthusiastically to Southey, 'Young Hazlitt has taken masterly Portraits of me & Wordsworth, very much in the manner of Titian's Portraits'.[56] This comparison suggests that this portrait may have been similar in conception to the one that Hazlitt did of Charles Lamb (NPG),[57] which also displays a Titian-like or Spanish manner. Hazlitt evidently thought this particularly appropriate for Coleridge, for he later recollected Coleridge's face as having 'a purple tinge as we see it in the pale and thoughtful complexions of the Spanish portrait-painters, Murillo and Velasquez.'[58] This effect was noted much later by a visitor to Coleorton in 1938 (when the house was about to be let and paintings were stacked against walls), who noted 'Coleridge by Hazlitt, rather "Spanish" looking'.[59]

After beginning his portraits of Coleridge and Wordsworth, Hazlitt went to Manchester and took both pictures with him, or so Coleridge conjectured in writing to the Beaumonts on 1 October 1803.[60] After the artist's return, Coleridge sat for him again on 27 October.[61] Perhaps it was at this point that Wordsworth withdrew from his part of the enterprise. He had paid Hazlitt

[54] For chronology, see Mark L. Reed, *Wordsworth: The Chronology of the Middle Years 1800–1815* (Cambridge, Mass.: Harvard University Press, 1975), 215; *CL* ii. 957–8, 960, 1004; *EY* 446–7 n., 593–4, 600; W. Carew Hazlitt, *Memoirs of William Hazlitt*, i. 103 n.

[55] *CL* ii. 958. [56] Ibid. 960.

[57] This picture, painted in the autumn of 1804, was subsequently owned by Coleridge who left it to James Gillman. See Mary Lamb's letter to Sara Fricker Coleridge dated 13 Oct. 1804 (*The Letters of Charles and Mary Lamb*, ed. E. W. Marrs, Jr. (Ithaca, NY: Cornell University Press, 1975), ii. 149), and *RP* i. 303.

[58] W. Hazlitt, 'My First Acquaintance with Poets', 109.

[59] Anonymous note in 'Notes on Collections', NPG Archive.

[60] *CL* ii. 1004. [61] *CN* i. 1619.

three guineas for his portrait, but he later wrote to Hazlitt's son William of the unsatisfactory outcome: 'I cannot recollect that I ever saw him but once since the year 1803 or 1804, when he passed some time in this neighbourhood. He was then practising portrait-painting; with professional views. At his desire, I sat to him, but as he did not satisfy himself or my friends, the unfinished work was destroyed.'[62] Coleridge, however, showed no sign of dissatisfaction, and Southey was probably echoing Coleridge's own view when he wrote to Richard Duppa on 14 December 1803, 'Haslitt [*sic*], whom you saw at Paris, has been here; a man of real genius. He has made a very fine picture of Coleridge for Sir George Beaumont, which is said to be in Titian's manner.'[63] This is also the first mention of Beaumont's having commissioned the picture, for which Coleridge himself had supposedly paid 'an unknown sum'[64] previously. As by this time it was known that Coleridge would be going abroad for his health, Beaumont probably wished to possess an image of the poet as a memento. He may therefore have taken over the commission from Coleridge, who is likely to have had second thoughts about his ability to spare the unknown sum he had paid.

Hazlitt's portrait, which had previously excited so much interest in Coleridge's circle, now stimulated his friends to find tropes for its deficiencies. Southey, who may not have seen the picture when he mentioned it previously, wrote to Coleridge on 11 June 1804, 'Hazlitt's does look as if you were on your trial, and certainly had stolen the horse; but then you did it so cleverly,—it had been a deep, well-laid scheme, and it was no fault of yours that you had been detected.'[65] A year or so later, Wordsworth

[62] 23 May 1831, *LY* pt. 2, pp. 476–7. I have changed 'I passed' in the first quoted sentence to 'he passed'; there is no MS source and the only printed source, the W. Carew Hazlitt *Memoirs*, i. 103 n., has 'he passed'.

[63] R. Southey, *Life and Correspondence*, ed. C. C. Southey (6 vols.; London: Longman, Brown, Green, & Longman, 1849–50), ii. 238.

[64] *EY* 446 n. *EY* 447 n. quotes Coleridge as writing of 'the money he [W. W.] and I . . . have paid [for the portraits'; however, the editor is mistaken in inferring that in 1805 Wordsworth possessed a portrait of Coleridge by Hazlitt; what Wordsworth had was an engraving after the Northcote portrait (see below).

[65] Southey, *Life and Correspondence*, ii. 291.

described the expression to Beaumont as 'quite dolorous and funereal',[66] while in an even more mournful vein, Dorothy Wordsworth wrote to Lady Beaumont that the portrait was 'so dismal that I shrink from the sight of it. I thought of Coleridge as dying, and not merely dying, but dying of sorrow and raised up upon his bed to take a last farewell of his Friends.'[67] These adverse reactions may indicate that Hazlitt spoiled the portrait by overpainting it, something that is certainly true of some of his surviving works.

After Hazlitt's hasty departure from the Lake District, Coleridge wrote to his wife in January 1804 about the pictures that had been left behind. 'As to that rude Sketch of my Face', he remarked, 'up in the upper Book room Garret, if you have no wish for it, & if on coming into the Country Sara Hutchinson should be at all pleased with it, as a rude sketch of me, it would gratify me that she should have it'.[68] This cannot refer to the picture done for Beaumont, which, whatever its peculiarities, was not a sketch. Evidently there was another portrait, perhaps not an independent design but a preparatory sketch for the finished picture. It may have been this sketch that Wordsworth had in mind over a decade later when he wrote to Charles Lamb of 'a Picture of Coleridge, now in existence at Keswick', and followed this with the sardonic remark, 'This piece of art is not producible for fear of fatal consequence to married Ladies, but is kept in a private room, as a special treat to those who may wish to sup upon horrors.'[69] As far as I have been able to ascertain, there are no further references to this picture by members of Coleridge's circle. Ironically, both of Hazlitt's depictions of Coleridge, so much discussed at the time of their execution, remain untraced.

By 1804 Coleridge had settled on going to Malta for his health, and the next two portraits, by George Dance and James Northcote (Cat. nos. 8 and 9), were commissioned by Sir George

[66] *EY*, 3 June 1805, p. 594. [67] 11 June 1805, *EY* 103.

[68] *CL* ii. 1025.

[69] Letter dated 21 Nov. 1816, *The Letters of William and Dorothy Wordsworth: A Supplement of New Letters*, ed. Alan G. Hill (Oxford: Clarendon, 1993), 161–2.

4. George Dance

Beaumont as mementos. Both were executed shortly before Coleridge's departure. Dance (1741–1825), a founding member of the Royal Academy, is remembered more as an architect—it was he who designed Sir George Beaumont's neo-Gothic mansion at Coleorton—than as a portrait artist, but he showed twenty-four portraits at the Royal Academy, and three at the Society of Artists during the period 1761–1800.[70] In 1809 he would publish *A Collection of Portraits Sketched from the Life Since the Year 1793*, two volumes of soft-ground etchings by William Daniell after Dance's designs, dedicated to Sir George Beaumont. Among the subjects, all shown in profile, were James Boswell, Sir William Chambers, and John Flaxman. Coleridge's portrait is not there but is basically similar, a lightly shaded line drawing, signed and dated 21 March 1804. The dark hair is long and the lips parted showing some upper teeth as in a number of other portraits. Southey found this representation remarkably unlike, drily remarking in his letter to Coleridge of 11 June 1804, 'Dance's drawing has that merit at least, that nobody would ever suspect you of having been the original.'[71] However, there is some resemblance between this drawing and the earlier Hancock portrait, both as to features and expression.

Before embarking for Malta, Coleridge stayed with Sir George Beaumont, sometimes at Beaumont's London residence and sometimes at his cottage at Dunmow in Essex.[72] Beaumont commissioned James Northcote (1746–1831) to execute a portrait shortly before the poet's departure. Northcote was known for history painting—particularly his paintings for Boydell's Shakespeare Gallery, such as his *Murder of the Little Princes in the Tower* ('King Edward V, and his Brother Richard, Duke of York, Murdered in the Tower by Order of Richard III'), as well as for portraiture. Once Reynolds's pupil and assistant, he exhibited prolifically at the Royal Academy—229 pictures from 1773 to 1828.[73] Among his recent successes had been portraits of William

[70] *Royal Academy*, ii. 239; *Dict.* 71.
[71] Southey, *Life and Correspondence*, ii. 291.
[72] See A. C. Sewter, 'Coleridge, Beaumont, and Coleorton', *Leicester and Rutland Magazine*, 1 (Dec. 1958), 30–5.
[73] See *Dict.* 205.

5. James Northcote

Godwin (1801–2) and of Edward Jenner (1803), both now in the National Portrait Gallery. If Coleridge had anything to do with the choice of artist, it may well be, as has been suggested, because Northcote claimed relationship with the Northcotes of Ottery St Mary and Coleridge's brother Frank had loved Maria Northcote of that family.[74] Northcote was reputed to pay little attention to drawing studies before painting,[75] and this may explain how he was able to produce a portrait with such extraordinary rapidity. Coleridge recorded in a Notebook 'Sunday, March 25th sate to Northcote for a Sketch, if possible, a Portrait of me for Sir G. Beaumont',[76] but the sitting must have terminated abruptly, because on that same day Coleridge wrote to Humphry Davy: 'I returned from Mr. Northcote's having been diseased by the change in the weather too grievously to permit me to consider sitting.'[77] Yet on the next day Joseph Farington dined at Northcote's and recorded that the picture was finished. 'Before dinner Northcote showed us a Head of Coleridge which He began yesterday & finished today. It is for Sir G. Beaumont and is very like.'[78] On the day following that (27 March) Coleridge was writing from Portsmouth on his way to Malta.

In Northcote's depiction Coleridge's expression has a dramatic, *sturm und drang* quality, accented by the contrast between his gleaming face and his dark clothing against a dark background. Evidently his black costume was a decade or so ahead of its time, for until Byron, according to Doris Langley Moore, black clothes were seldom worn except by mourners, clergymen, and members of the legal profession, and Byron's choice of black was 'a major contribution to costume history'.[79] (As Thomas

[74] See James Engell, *Coleridge: The Early Family Letters* (Oxford: Clarendon, 1994), 9, 56 n.

[75] R. and S. Redgrave, *A Century of British Painters* (Ithaca, NY: Cornell University Press), 121–2, also states he neglected the preparation of his grounds.

[76] *CN* ii. 1976. [77] *CL* ii. 110.

[78] *The Diary of Joseph Farington*, ed. Kenneth Garlick and Angus Macintyre (New Haven and London: Yale University Press, 1979), vi. 2227.

[79] D. L. Moore, 'Byronic Dress', *Costume*, 5 (1971), 6–7.

Colley Grattan would point out after meeting Coleridge much later, the poet was ever partial to black clothing and had described himself as dressed 'all in black' on the Hamburg packet in 1798.[80]) In Northcote's rendering the familiar parted lips and visible front teeth contribute to the impression of emotional intensity. A faint dew of perspiration appears on his forehead and at the end of his nose, and light reflects from these prominent features. This is the first Coleridge portrait in which the subject's head appears distinctly round; his ruddy-cheeked face even seems puffy, his hair is cut short, and a gleam in each of his dark gray eyes makes them appear to be wildly staring. Kathleen Coburn speculated that some of these details might be related to a contemporary Notebook entry about the effects of opium taken in daytime: 'the puffing Asthma, eye closing, & startlings'.[81] This idea can also be supported by the glistening of the skin in the Northcote portrait. A mutual friend told Thomas De Quincey that she always knew when Coleridge was under the influence 'by the glistening of his cheeks'. De Quincey continues:

> Coleridge's face, as is well known to his acquaintances, exposed a large surface of cheek; too large for the intellectual expression of his features generally, had not the final effect been redeemed by what Wordsworth styled his 'godlike forehead.' The result was that no possible face so broadly betrayed and published any effects whatever, especially these lustrous effects from excesses in opium. For some years I failed to consider reflectively, or else, reflecting, I failed to decipher, this resplendent acreage of cheek. But at last, either *proprio marte*, or prompted by some medical hint, I came to understand that the glistening face, glorious from afar like the old Pagan face of the demigod Æsculapius, simply reported the gathering accumulation of insensible perspiration.[82]

[80] See Thomas Colley Grattan, *Beaten Paths and Those Who Trod Them* (London: Chapman & Hall, 1862), ii. 108. Coleridge's description of himself dressed in black, dancing (*BL* ii. 161) features prominently in Wallace Stevens's 'The Figure of the Youth as a Virile Poet', *The Necessary Angel* (London: Faber & Faber, 1959), 41.

[81] *CN* ii. 1977 (the entry immediately following the one noting his sitting for Northcote).

[82] De Quincey, *Confessions of an English Opium-Eater*, in *Collected Writings*, iii. 423. I thank Grevel Lindop for calling this passage to my attention.

6. James Northcote, replica (slightly cropped)

7. William Say, engraving after James Northcote

After the portrait was completed, Coleridge and his friends set about making copies available. On 29 March 1804 Coleridge wrote to Daniel Stuart: 'Northcote told me, that he could get his portrait of me admirably *copied* for 4 or 5 guineas: & I being exceedingly desirous that my Friends in the North should possess a likeness of me, in case of my Death, have authorized him to have it copied, if it continues to be admired as much as it has been, & if he in conscience can rely on the Artist for a Copy strictly honorable to the original, even tho' the original should be lost'.[83] In that event, Northcote was to give the artist a check for five guineas drawn on Stuart. At least one oil copy (Cat. No. 9A) was made, probably by Northcote himself. In this picture, somewhat rougher than the first, Coleridge's eyes are olive-green. A fine mezzotint was also engraved after the original, whose dramatic counterpoint of dark and light lent itself admirably to the mezzotint process, by William Say in 1805.[84] However, neither the original nor its reproductions continued to be admired, at least not by some of those who knew Coleridge best. After seeing Northcote's painting exhibited at the Royal Academy exhibition of 1804, Southey had written to Coleridge that 'this portrait by Northcote looks like a grinning idiot; and the worst is, that it is just enough like to pass for a good likeness, with those who know your features only imperfectly'.[85] The Say engraving fared no better with him. 'Sir George Beaumont', he wrote to John Rickman on 1 May 1805, 'has sent me down a print of Coleridge, which if it resembles any one, has a distant likeness to Count Burnetski, having exactly his eyes and hair'.[86] The Wordsworths' view was expressed diplomatically in a letter from William to Sir George Beaumont dated 3 June 1805, thanking Beaumont for 'your most acceptable present of Coleridge's portrait' (evidently the Say engraving):

[83] *CL* ii. 1113.

[84] It was published 20 Apr. 1805 by the engraver, 92 Norton Street, Mary-le-bon. Later, the *European Magazine* for Aug. 1819 published an engraving by J. Thomson based on Say's.

[85] 11 June 1804, Southey, *Life and Correspondence*, ii. 291.

[86] Southey, *Selections from the Letters*, ed. J. Warter (London: Longman, Brown, Green & Longman, 1856), i. 321. 'Count Burnetski' was Southey's cognomen for their mutual friend and former fellow Pantisocrat George Burnett.

It is as good a likeness as I expect to see of Coleridge [wrote William Wordsworth], taking it all together for I consider C.'s as a face absolutely impracticable. Mrs Wordsworth was overjoy'd at the sight of the Print, Dorothy and I much pleased. We think it excellent about the eyes and forehead which are the finest parts of C——'s face, and the general contour of the face is well given; but to my Sister and me, it seems to fail sadly about the middle of the face, particularly at the bottom of the nose: Mrs. W—— feels this also; and my Sister so much, that, except when she covers the whole of the middle of the face it seems to her so entirely to alter the expression, as rather to confound than revive in her mind the remembrance of the original. We think as far as mere likeness goes, Hazlitt's is better; but the expression in Hazlitt's is quite dolorous and funereal, that in this, much more pleasing though certainly far below what one would wish to see infused into a picture of C.[87]

Despite Wordsworth's gratitude, he makes it clear that the portrait fails to achieve the object of making the absent present, which was after all the purpose of the portraits executed before Coleridge went to Malta. On 11 June 1805, Dorothy Wordsworth endorsed this view, writing to Lady Beaumont: 'My Sister's pleasure at the first sight of the paint was equal to what the painter himself, I think could have desired; but the whole face, when seen all at once, seems to me scarcely to resemble Coleridge, though the forehead and outline of the shape of the face are very like him.'[88] Much later, Wordsworth bluntly described Northcote's painting as 'a poor performance'.[89] Although Northcote's is a striking painting, in the face of such criticism it must be considered less than successful as a portrait.

1806–1815

No portraits of Coleridge were taken in Malta, but a highly memorable one (Cat. no. 10), despite its incomplete state, was painted in Italy by Washington Allston in 1806. The artist and

87 *EY* 593–4. 88 *EY* 600.

89 Letter to an unknown correspondent, dated 2 Jan. 1847, *LY* pt. 4, p. 827.

8. Washington Allston

Coleridge developed a close friendship during Coleridge's time in Rome, as can be seen in Allston's tender recollection of those days:

He used to call Rome the *silent* city; but I could never think of it as such, while with him; for, meet him when, or where I would, the fountain of his mind was never dry, but like the far-reaching aqueducts that once supplied the mistress of the world, its living stream seemed specially to flow for every classic ruin over which we wandered. And when I recall some of our walks under the pines of the Villa Borghese, I am almost tempted to dream, that I once listened to Plato, in the groves of the Academy.[90]

Coleridge was also deeply impressed by Allston. He later called him a man of 'high and rare genius' and characterized him with great critical acuity as 'a Painter born to renew the 15th Century'.[91] Allston had learned much from the artists of the Italian Renaissance, especially Titian, about the mixing of colours and glazing, as can be seen in his exciting painting of 1805, *Diana and Her Nymphs in the Chase* (Fogg Art Museum), whose 'divine semitransparent and grey-green Light' Coleridge evoked at length in a Notebook description.[92] The particular effects of this first Allston portrait of Coleridge are well described by Edgar Preston Richardson:

The whole picture becomes a single sensation of light and color, within whose harmony the eye later picks out the blended notes. The cool sil-

[90] Undated letter quoted by William Dunlap, *History of the Arts of Design in the United States* (New York, 1834), vol. ii., pt. 2, p. 167. The correspondent is not identified but it may have been Dunlap himself. This is the earliest source for Allston's letter; the location of the MS is unknown. The passage was later printed with minor variants, the most important of which is 'stream' for 'streams', by Jared B. Flagg, *The Life and Letters of Washington Allston* (New York: Charles Scribner's Sons, 1892), 64. For the dates of Coleridge's association with Allston in Italy, see Donald Sultana, *Samuel Taylor Coleridge in Malta and Italy* (Oxford: Basil Blackwell, 1969), 388–94.

[91] Letter to C. R. Leslie, Feb. 1822, *CL* v. 208); marginal note next to Allston's poem 'America to Great Britain', in Coleridge's own copy of *Sibylline Leaves*, once the property of Henry Wadsworth Longfellow and now in the Houghton Library (kindly verified by Jennie Rathbun). The notation was first published, to my best knowledge, by M. F. Sweetser in his *Allston* (Boston: Houghton, Osgood, & Co., 1879).

[92] *CN* ii. 2831.

ver flesh tone, the cool white, black, and gray of the costume and background, are varied only by the warm brown vertical band at the right. The head is brushed in very broadly. Separate tones like the cool rose of the lips and cheeks exist as part of the whole . . . The luminosity, the inner vitality, the spiritual solitude of the dreaming head, and the vivid quality of first impression in a sketch combine to make this a remarkable image of the romantic poet.[93]

As has also been suggested, Allston's own *Self-Portrait*, a Romantic icon showing the artist musing in the caves of the Vatican, is similar to the Coleridge portrait in tone and size, to such an extent that 'they may be thought of perhaps as pendants, a commemoration of a newly formed but already intense personal relationship'.[94] Coleridge considered Allston's portrait of him the best to date, as expressed in a letter to Sir George Beaumont dated 7 December 1811.[95] The picture was to remain unfinished, as a result of Coleridge's suddenly leaving Rome to escape the real or imagined threat of Napoleon to him. Although Allston himself returned to England in 1808, his portrait of Coleridge remained with some cases that were not shipped until 1815 and was later brought by him to America when Allston repatriated himself in 1818. Consequently, this picture was so little known in Coleridge's circle that after his death Henry Nelson Coleridge confused an account of it with Allston's much better-known portrait of 1814 and puzzled over the seeming disparity between Coleridge's appearance in the latter and his age at the time of the painting of what was actually the former.[96] In a poem written in the mid-twentieth century, Robert Lowell described a reproduction of the 1806 portrait as a reflection of Coleridge's psychological problems and opium addiction, with his gaze 'paranoid,

[93] E. P. Richardson, *Washington Allston* (Chicago: University of Chicago Press, 1948), 77–8.

[94] W. H. Gerdts and T. E. Stebbins, '*A Man of Genius*' (Boston: Museum of Fine Arts, 1979), 50.

[95] *CL* iii. 351.

[96] These remarks appear in the biographical supplement at the end of vol. ii of the important second edition of *BL* edited by HNC and SC and published in 1847. From the internal arrangement of the supplement, it appears that this part of the text was HNC's, but SC would not have known any more about this subject.

inert', and 'his eyes lost in flesh, lips baked and black'.[97] However, the subject's lips are not black in the original: it may have been its unfinished nature that, with his own knowledge of Coleridge's story, led Lowell so to interpret it, making the poet a version of his own Ancient Mariner—who had been one of those who suffered 'with black lips baked'[98]—back from his sea voyage. The detail of 'eyes lost in flesh' is not true of this painting either, but is another deliberate echo, this time of the reaction of one who knew Coleridge's face well and was shocked at how he looked upon his return from Malta and Italy in the autumn of 1806.

'His fatness has quite changed him,' wrote Dorothy Wordsworth, '—it is more like the flesh of a person in dropsy than one in health; his eyes . . . are lost in it . . .'; and she could find only a faint and transitory shadow of the former 'divine expression of his countenance'.[99] When Thomas De Quincey first met Coleridge in the summer of the following year, he too noticed the poet's corpulence but found his expression poetic.

> In height he might seem to be about five feet eight (he was, in reality about an inch and a-half taller, but his figure was of an order which drowns the height); his person was broad and full, and tended even to corpulence; his complexion was fair, though not what painters technically style fair, because it was associated with black hair; his eyes were large, and soft in their expression; and it was from the peculiar appearance of haze or dreaminess which mixed with their light that I recognized my object.[100]

The contrast may perhaps be accounted for by the difference between one who had known Coleridge in his original brightness

[97] R. Lowell, 'To Delmore Schwartz', *Life Studies*, 2nd edn. (London: Faber & Faber, 1968), 67. Although the artist is not named, the poem says the subject is 'Coleridge, back from Malta,' and the 1806 Allston portrait is the only one that could be so characterized.

[98] 'The Rime of the Ancient Mariner', *Poems*, ed. John Beer (London: J. M. Dent, rev. edn. 1993), p. 225, ll. 157, 163. In 'To Delmore Schwartz' the role of the Albatross is taken by a stuffed duck that had been Schwartz's 'first kill', and its 'lubricious, drugged' stare parallels Coleridge's.

[99] Letter to Catherine Clarkson, 6 Nov. 1806, *MY* i. 87.

[100] De Quincey, 'Samuel Taylor Coleridge', *Collected Writings*, ii. 150. This essay was one of four which were originally published in *Tait's Edinburgh Magazine* in 1834–5.

and one who saw him for the first time; it must also be remembered that De Quincey was writing some twenty-eight years after the event. (He was mistaken about Coleridge's height, which by De Quincey's own account was measured as five feet ten inches by Benjamin Robert Haydon in 1810.)[101] Certainly little in Coleridge's external circumstances in 1807 can account for an improvement in the appearance of the outward man. However, it does seem as if Coleridge's personal appearance could vary dramatically within short periods, and this may have been one of the effects of his opium addiction. Robert Southey recognized this phenomenon in a remarkable letter to the next artist to paint Coleridge's portrait.

Mathilda Betham, a poet as well as an artist, was the daughter of the Revd William Betham, clergyman and schoolmaster in Suffolk, and author of genealogical works. One of the poems in her first book of verse, *Elegies* (1797), had prompted a poem from Coleridge, 'To Matilda Betham from a Stranger'.[102] Though self-taught as an artist, she gained some professional recognition, exhibiting two pictures at the Royal Academy in 1807–8 and at least one at the British Institution in 1811. The idea of a portrait of Coleridge could have been initiated by Coleridge's friend George Dyer, whose portrait Betham had painted and who had made the arrangements for her portrait of Southey.[103] On 3 April 1808 Coleridge wrote to Betham at 14 New Cavendish Street to confirm arrangements, adding the disclaimer '. . . Though my poor face is a miserable subject for a painter (for in honest truth I am what the world calls, and with more truth than usual, an *ugly* fellow) . . .'.[104] In May 1808 Coleridge wrote to her again, apologizing for his failure to keep an appointment to sit.[105] It was once assumed that Betham did not finish this portrait until she visited

[101] 'Postscript' to 'Coleridge and Opium Eating', *Collected Writings*, v. 213.

[102] *CPW* i. 374–6. See my 'Coleridge's "To Matilda Betham, from a Stranger" ', *The Wordsworth Circle*, 27 (1996), 169–72.

[103] See Charles and Mary Lamb, *Letters*, ii. 275, 277 n.; Southey, *Letters*, ii. 67. Southey referred to Dyer as 'Miss Betham's agent' in a letter to John Rickman dated 6 May 1808.

[104] *CL* iii. 83. [105] Ibid. 99–101.

the Lake District in the summer and early autumn of 1809, when she painted miniatures of the Southeys, Sara Fricker Coleridge, and the young Sara Coleridge.[106] However, Coleridge's portrait (Cat. no. 11) must have been ready, as Kathleen Coburn points out,[107] before its subject left London in June or July, since an engraving after it was featured in *The Cabinet, a Monthly Magazine of Polite Literature* for February 1809.[108] This representation of Coleridge accompanied an anonymous article, 'Samuel Taylor Coleridge, Esq.', which discussed the poet's early pro-Revolutionary sentiments and his 'sloth-jaundiced disposition', and recommended to him 'a regular employment of six hours in the day'.[109]

Under the impression that the portrait was yet to be painted, Southey wrote to Betham on July 2, 1808, giving an unusually interesting description of her subject:

> You would have found him the most wonderful man living in conversation, but the most impracticable one for a painter, and had you begun the picture it is ten thousand to one that you must have finished it from memory. His countenance is the most variable that I have ever seen; sometimes it is kindled with the brightest expression, and sometimes all its light goes out, and is utterly extinguished. Nothing can convey stronger indications of power than his eye, eyebrow, and forehead. Nothing can be more imbecile than all the rest of the face; look at them separately, you would hardly think it possible that they could belong to one head; look at them together, you would wonder how they came so, and are puzzled what to expect from a character whose outward and visible signs are so contradictory.[110]

Here we have independent corroboration of Coleridge's own feeling, as expressed in his letter to John Thelwall among others,

[106] See Molly Lefebure, *The Bondage of Love* (London: Gollancz, 1986), 276 n., portrait of Sara Fricker Coleridge reproduced as frontispiece (also in Holmes, *Coleridge: Early Visions* (London: Hodder & Stoughton, 1989), 112–13), and portrait of little Sara facing p. 181.

[107] *CL* iii. 4049 n. [108] NS 1/2.

[109] The poem addressed to Coleridge's brother George ('To the Rev. George Coleridge'), first published in the *Poems* of 1797, was reprinted entire.

[110] From Ernest Betham, *A House of Letters*, 2nd edn. (London: Jarrold & Sons, ?1905), 110.

9. Mathilda Betham

that the lower parts of his face were problematic and posed a special problem for portrait artists. The Northcote portrait, as we have seen, had disappointed Coleridge's friends because of its failure to cope with this area adequately. Betham addressed this difficulty in her own way. She presented a delicate image, the lips thick but only slightly opened, the face fleshy but not fat. As in the Allston portrait, the dark brown, natural hair is shorter than in pre-Malta depictions of Coleridge, and there are faint sideburns. But the most striking feature is the contemplative look of the large, grey eyes. The poet wears a dark coat and white cravat, bringing his face and neck forward against a dark background. E. H. Coleridge, in his MS Notes, found it 'difficult even in the photograph from the original miniature to trace any likeness to Coleridge' but it must be remembered that, born in 1846, he had never seen his grandfather. Of necessity he based his judgement on the portraits he knew, and he knew of no other for the eight-year period after Northcote's and before Dawe's. While it is true that Betham's respect for Coleridge bordered on awe, and that this could have led her to somewhat idealize the image of the poet, her rendering is enough like Allston's (which she could not have seen) and enough like De Quincey's description to suggest that this is a reliable representation of Coleridge in 1808, perceptively rendered as both introspective and sensuous.

Coleridge's next portraitist was a far better-known artist, George Dawe. Dawe, then an Associate Member of the Royal Academy, had won that institution's gold medal in 1803 and would become a full member in 1814. He exhibited prolifically in the annual exhibitions from 1804 to 1818, showing mostly portraits but also some history paintings.[111] In 1811 he took a plaster cast of Coleridge's head as the basis for a ceramic bust, and he also did a portrait drawing in crayon (Cat. nos. 12, 13, and 14). The cast pleased Coleridge so much that he sent it (or a duplicate) to Sir George Beaumont, writing on 7 December 1811: 'Mr Dawe, Royal Associate, who plaistered my face for me, says that he

[111] See *Royal Academy*, ii. 272–3.

never saw so excellent a Mask, and so unaffected by any expression of Pain or Uneasiness. On Tuesday at the farthest, a Cast will be finished which I was vain enough to desire to be packed up and sent to Dunmow . . .'.[112] Coleridge's friend Henry Crabb Robinson, who saw the cast in the following year, concurred: 'Called . . . on Dawe, who has formed a very fine cast from Coleridge's head. His forehead and eyebrows are singularly striking, and I was never before so impressed with the power expressed in his countenance . . .'[113] The sitter was pleased with Dawe's drawing as well, for he sent it too to Beaumont, characterizing it as 'a chalk drawing of my face which I think far more like than any former attempt, excepting Allston's full length Portrait of me . . .'[114]

The Dawe portrait consists of two parts, being a sketch of the head added to a sheet on which the figure was then drawn.[115] It is a good example of George Stanley's judgement that 'His portraits are reckoned good likenesses of the persons, but not expressive of character.'[116] A portly Coleridge is seated on a Chippendale chair, his eyes slightly upraised as if in meditation. This is not so much the poet as the Coleridge who delivered three series of lectures in 1811–12: he holds a book open with the index finger of his left hand, and there are seven more books on a table

[112] *CL* iii. 351. No reference to the existence of the Dawe life-mask has been made since Robinson's admiring comment, but it appears very likely that either the original or a cast taken from it found its way to Boston by 1835 and is now in the collection of the Warren Anatomical Museum, Harvard Medical School. See Supplementary Note A, 'Coleridge Masks in the Warren Anatomical Museum'.

[113] 4 Apr. 1812. *Henry Crabb Robinson on Books and Their Writers*, ed. Edith J. Morley (3 vols.; London: J. M. Dent, 1938), i. 68.

[114] The letter continues: 'which with all his casts, &c. . . . are lying at Leghorn—with no chance of procuring them' (*CL* iii. 351). Evidently Coleridge misremembered Allston's half-length portrait executed in Rome (see above) as full-length. Allston embarked for England from Leghorn in March 1808, but according to Nathalia Wright, some of his cases were left behind and the portrait, in one of these, did not reach England until the summer of 1815. See *The Correspondence of Washington Allston*, ed. N. Wright (Lexington, Ky.: University Press of Kentucky, 1993), 56 n. 11.

[115] See Lord Coleridge, *The Story of a Devonshire House* (London: T. Fisher Unwin, 1905), 11.

[116] Michael Bryan, *Biographical and Critical Dictionary of Painters and Engravers*, rev. and enlarged by George Stanley (London: H. S. Bohn, 1853), 205.

10. George Dawe

in front of him, with still more below. Two of the books on the table are lettered on their spines 'Platon vol VII' and 'Platon vol VIII'. This picture was intended as part of a larger project: as the poet put it in a letter to Mrs Coleridge on 21 April 1812, 'Dawe and I will be of mutual service to each other'.[117] This mutual service was to include a portrait engraving that Coleridge anticipated in a Notebook entry of March 1812,[118] headed 'Proposals for publishing a Print of S. T. Coleridge, Esqr from a half-length picture painted by G. Dawe'. It was to be a sizeable print, 20 × 15 in., priced at one guinea, with proofs to be sold at two guineas. As Dawe was a mezzotint engraver as well as a painter, it is likely that he was to reproduce the drawing himself. This plan may have been associated with the 1812 republication of *The Friend*,[119] but the list headed 'Subscribers names' is a blank, and the Dawe portrait was not to be reproduced graphically until long after Coleridge's death, in Leopold Lowenstam's fine etching of *c.*1870. Another 'mutual service' may have been the illustration of a Coleridge poem, which the poet reported on enthusiastically in his letter of 7 December 1811 to Beaumont: 'Dawe is engaged on a picture (the figures about 4 feet) from my poem of LOVE'; and after quoting lines 13–16, 65, and 99, he remarked 'His sketch is very beautiful & has more expression than I ever found in his former productions—except indeed his Imogen.'[120]

Dawe's drawing, painting, and bust were all exhibited at the Royal Academy exhibition of 1812,[121] and Coleridge remained very hopeful. In the letter to Mrs Coleridge to which reference has already been made, Coleridge remarked: 'The Bust & the Picture from Genevieve are at the R. Academy, & are already

[117] *CL* iii. 386. [118] *CN* iii. 4143.

[119] As Kathleen Coburn (*CN* iii. 4143 n.) suggests.

[120] Exhibited at the RA in 1812 (see below) and at the British Institution in 1813, the present whereabouts of this painting are unknown. The whereabouts of the bust are also unknown. In 1815, it was in the possession of John Morgan, who in a letter to William Hood on 10 Aug. suggested that an engraving be executed after it in connection with the publication of *BL*. (See letter printed in *BL*, app. C, ii. 284.) Despite Morgan's urging Hood again on 17 Aug. (*BL* ii. 285–6), even sending Dawe's address, no engraving is known to have been executed.

[121] Nos. 547, 220, and 922 respectively.

talked of'.[122] All three were puffed in Daniel Stuart's *Courier*, with which Coleridge was closely connected as a journalist, for 4 May 1812: 'Mr. Dawe has a large picture from Coleridge's poem of 'Love,' and a spirited chalk drawing of Mr. Coleridge, together with a bust of great merit.'[123] The *Genevieve* picture was puffed again in the *Courier* for 15 August, and it was also shown at the British Institution, but the general reaction appears to have been negative. According to William T. Whitley, 'The picture [*Genevieve*] was not admired, and still less were Dawe's presentiments of the poet.'[124] The *St James Chronicle* commented 'The portrait is but indifferent, but it is better than the bust, which is absolutely disagreeable.'[125] This contemporary response matches Charles Lamb's general judgement of Dawe: 'With such guides ['the Hopners, and the Lawrences'] he struggled on through laborious nights and days, till he reached the eminence he aimed at—of mediocrity.'[126] Later, perhaps because of Dawe's closeness in matters of money,[127] Coleridge became very hostile to Dawe, referred to him as 'the Grub', and actually wrote a nasty epigram after being stopped to let Dawe's funeral cortège pass by. None the less, we would not like to do without this portrait, which according to E. H. Coleridge 'was, in the late Lord Coleridge's opinion, a most characteristic likeness of his uncle'.[128] As John Duke Coleridge had a clear recollection of the poet, this

[122] *CL* iii. 386.

[123] See David V. Erdman, 'Unrecorded Coleridge Variants', *Studies in Bibliography*, 11 (1958), 160–1.

[124] W. T. Whitley, *Art in England 1800–1820* (Cambridge: Cambridge University Press, 1928), 201. According to Morgan's letters to William Hood cited above, the bust was 'a very fine one as to expression', but 'in baking the Bust, the Forehead shrunk a little' (*BL* ii. 284, 286).

[125] 4–6 June 1812. Quoted by Whitley, *Art in England 1800–1820*, 201, without any indication of the source, which is given in the *Whitley Papers* (BM Dept. of Prints and Drawings), s. v. Dawe.

[126] C. and M. Lamb, 'Recollections of a late R. A.', *Works*, ed. E. V. Lucas (London: Dent & Methuen, 1903–5), i. 331–6.

[127] As suggested by Coburn, *CN* iii. 4142 n.

[128] S. T. Coleridge, *Letters*, ed. E. H. Coleridge (London: Heinemann, 1895), i. 572. 'The family likeness', wrote EHC in his MS Notes, 'here appears for the first time. I can trace looks of my father, of the late John Taylor Coleridge, and others . . .'

testimony is important.[129] The Dawe portrait is, furthermore, the sole firsthand visual representation of Coleridge for the five-year period 1809–13.

Coleridge and Washington Allston met again in Bristol in 1813, and their friendship was immediately renewed. Allston was at the time preparing for a one-man exhibition at the Merchant Taylors Hall, while Coleridge was preparing two series of lectures, one on literature, the other on the French Revolution and its aftermath. Each produced a work that was, as it were, a commemoration of their relationship. Coleridge began an essay that was initially to have promoted Allston's exhibition but became the more general 'On the Principles of Genial Criticism', in which Coleridge declared that Allston's 'great picture [*The Dead Man Restored*], with his Hebe, landscape, and sea-piece, would of themselves suffice to elucidate the fundamental doctrines of color, ideal form, and grouping . . .'[130] Allston for his part painted at the home of Coleridge's Bristol friend Josiah Wade what was to become the most celebrated of the Coleridge life portraits.

Coleridge's account of the second Allston portrait (Cat. no. 15) features the now almost to be expected deprecation of his own face:

Of my own portrait I am no judge—Allston is highly gratified with it . . . I am not *mortified*, tho' I own I should better like it to be otherwise, that my face is not a manly or representable Face—Whatever is impressive, is part fugitive, part *existent* only in the imaginations of persons impressed strongly by my conversation. The face *itself* is a FEEBLE, unmanly face . . . The exceeding *weakness*, Strengthlessness, in my face was ever painful to me—not as my own face—but as *a* face . . . On

[129] On 20 May 1893 Lord Coleridge wrote to EHC: 'Coleridge died when I was a boy of thirteen. When I saw him most frequently I was between seven and nine years old, and I suppose I never was in his company above seven or eight times in all': E. H. Coleridge, *Letters and Correspondence of John Duke Lord Coleridge* (London: William Heinemann, 1904), ii. 378.

[130] S. T. Coleridge, *Shorter Works and Fragments*, ed. H. J. Jackson and J. R. de J. Jackson (Princeton: Princeton University Press, 1995), i. 360–1. *Hebe* is untraced; the sea-piece is identified by the editors as *The Rising of a Thunderstorm at Sea* (Museum of Fine Arts, Boston).

11. Washington Allston

Wednesday Allston is to finish my face—& he will require two Sittings after that—I trust Thursday and Saturday . . .'[131]

After the portrait was finished, Allston added it to the one-man exhibition he already had under way, probably as a companion to another tribute of friendship, his portrait of Dr John King (Fine Arts Museums of San Francisco). Allston stated of these two pictures, 'I have painted but few portraits, and I think these are my best.'[132] This portrait became the favourite among Coleridge's circle. Sara Coleridge later wrote: 'Allston's portrait is the best that has been taken of my Father,' and Henry Nelson Coleridge called it 'the best portrait of my late Uncle'.[133] According to William Wordsworth, 'It is the only likeness of the great original that ever gave me the least pleasure; and it is, in fact, most happily executed, as everyone who has a distinct remembrance of what C. was at that time must with delight acknowledge, and would be glad to certify.'[134] It was at least in part the idealization of Allston's Coleridge that captivated the poet's admirers. 'It embodies,' wrote Joseph Henry Green, 'as far as can be presented to the senses, the character of the poet as the philosopher with the seraph's wing.'[135]

Interestingly, it was Allston himself who expressed an important reservation. In a letter to Henry Hope Reed, Wordsworth's American editor, the artist remarked:

So far as I can judge of my own production, the likeness is a true one; but it is Coleridge in repose; and, though not unstirred by the perpetual ground-swell of his <ever-act> ever-working intellect, and shadowing forth something of the deep Philosopher, it is not Coleridge in his *highest* mood, the poetic state. When in that state, no face that I ever saw was like to his: it seemed almost <intellect> *spirit made visible*, without a

[131] Letter to J. J. Morgan, 16 Aug. 1814, *CL* vi. 29–30.

[132] See Flagg, *Allston*, 104.

[133] *Sara Coleridge and Henry Reed*, ed. Broughton, 85; letter to John Murray, 22 Dec. 1834 (John Murray Archive).

[134] Wordsworth, letter to John Peace, 12 Dec. 1842, *LY*, pt. 4, p. 394.

[135] Quoted by Flagg from a letter to Richard Henry Dana, Snr. (n.d.), *Allston*, 107. See *Correspondence of Washington Allston*, 552. Flagg himself thought the picture portrayed 'the delicate feeling of his feminine gentleness with masculine thought', *Allston*, 107.

shadow of the physical upon it. Could I have *then* fixed it upon canvass—but it was beyond the reach of *my* art.[136]

Indeed, the artist developed what can almost be called an obsession with the two different aspects of Coleridge's face, later expressing himself similarly on the subject in letters to William Dunlap (first published in Dunlap's *Rise and Progress*, 1834)[137] and in conversation to Bronson Alcott. After a meeting with Allston in Cambridgeport, Massachusetts, on 13 January 1835, Alcott wrote in his journal:

He said there could not be conceived a greater difference in the appearance of the countenance of Coleridge than during the times of conversation and of thought. When absorbed in meditation 'the outward man,' to use his expression, 'seemed to be a corpse. The eyes were inverted, as it were, and turned inward; the under lip fell, and the general expression of the countenance was that of idiocy, so entirely was the soul withdrawn from the external world and the animal functions. But the appearance of a friend, a stranger, a human being seemed to awake him from this exterior sleep; the eyes radiated supernatural splendor, the mouth was full of meaning, and the whole countenance was, perhaps, more purely angelic than that of any modern living man. He gave us the idea of a seraph more fully than had been given in others.'[138]

The language the artist employs in expressing his exalted view of Coleridge's 'poetic state' shows something of the affinity between Allston and Coleridge, and the 1814 portrait indeed conveys something of Coleridge's idealized self. Seated in a chair, he is shown three-quarter-length, his blue-grey eyes upraised as if meditatively, as in Dawe's drawing. The lips, always a peril for

[136] Letter to Henry Hope Reed, 13 June 1843, *Correspondence of Washington Allston*, 512–13. An edited version of this letter was printed in the pamphlet promoting subscriptions for the Cousins mezzotint (see below).

[137] See letter to William Dunlap conjecturally dated *c.*18 Feb. 1834, *Correspondence of Washington Allston*, 353.

[138] Amos Bronson Alcott, *The Journals of Bronson Alcott*, ed. Odell Shephard (Boston: Little, Brown, 1938), 54. It is interesting, that in a letter already quoted in this discussion, Coleridge himself wrote 'my face, unless when animated by immediate eloquence, expresses great Sloth, & great, indeed almost ideotic good nature' (*CL* i. 155–6).

Coleridge's artists, are closed and downturned, making the expression very serious. The right hand is tucked into his jacket; in the left he holds a silver snuffbox (which would reappear in the Phillips portrait), and a handkerchief (which would not) spreads on to his lap. Light shines on his face from an unseen source. The Gothic interior, with its ogee arch, lancet windows, and sculpture in a corbel, conveys a sense of the spiritual. Outside, the sky suggests either early morning or, more probably, dusk. In the dark interior (which may perhaps be meant to suggest St Mary Redcliffe, Bristol), Coleridge, as Gerdts and Stebbins remark, 'appears to radiate light from within'.[139] The figure in the corbel, seen in profile wearing a stocking cap, has impressed some as a representation of Chaucer,[140] which would intensify the medievalism of the scene. Just a few years earlier, William Blake had painted his *Sir Jeffrey Chaucer and the nine and twenty Pilgrims on their journey to Canterbury*,[141] showing a pensive Chaucer at the rear of a procession passing through a Gothic archway richly adorned with sculpture. Both pictures are very much of their time in associating medieval architecture and statuary with spirituality, and if Allston intended the statue to represent Chaucer, the link suggested between Coleridge and the fourteenth-century poet would parallel the link Blake implies between Chaucer's art and his own.

After Coleridge's death, members of his circle made efforts to reproduce Allston's highly impressive portrait. On 16 April 1836 Henry Nelson Coleridge wrote to Thomas Poole expressing the hope that Josiah Wade would permit 'the Bristol artist to whom you refer' (probably Thomas Curnock) to copy the picture, and on 1 September Poole reported:

> The Painter has finished my Copy, and I think has succeeded very well—It was exhibited, and I observe attracted much attention, at the British Institution, during the Late Meeting—I shall have it home soon,

[139] Gerdts and Stebbins, '*A Man of Genius*', 85.

[140] See e.g. *RP* i. 119.

[141] The painting (Pollok House, Glasgow) was executed in 1808, Blake's engraving after it in 1810.

and I hope you and Sara will *make* an opportunity of seeing it, and judge if you and Mr. Green would like a copy as you mentioned. Wade kindly says the Painter may command his drawing-room as long as is necessary.—The Painter has raised his Price to £7–0–0 . . .'[142]

According to Mrs Sandford, who considered the original as 'the only good portrait of S. T. Coleridge in existence', Poole's copy hung in the antechamber to his bookroom at Nether Stowey.[143] This copy (in which Coleridge's figure has, perhaps deliberately, been made less portly) is now in the collection at the Coleridge Cottage in Nether Stowey.[144] The projected copy for Green was evidently made as well, for there is another copy of the Allston portrait at Jesus College. Efforts by members of Coleridge's circle to perpetuate Allston's image of the poet did not stop with the copies. In 1853, ten years after Allston's death, Henry Crabb Robinson, according to whom his picture had 'great beauty more expressive of the poet's tenderness than power', joined a committee to get an engraving published.[145] Allston had once called the head of James Northcote that was reproduced as the frontispiece to Hazlitt's *Conversations of James Northcote, Esq., R. A.* (1830) 'one of the finest engraved portraits I have seen' and had expressed the wish that his Coleridge portrait be engraved by the same engraver.[146] That engraver was Thomas Wright (1792–1849), who was no longer living in 1853. It is likely that Allston would have approved of the choice of Samuel Cousins (1801–87) as the engraver, for he had once hoped that Cousins

[142] BL Add. MSS 35344 fos. 127, 129. However, the British Institution exhibition catalogue for 1836 does not list any such painting, nor does the one for 1835.

[143] Sandford, *Thomas Poole and His Friends*, ii. 317. Mrs Sandford names Curnock as the copyist.

[144] See *Coleridge Bulletin*, 7 (1996), 64.

[145] 7 June 1853. See *Henry Crabb Robinson*, ed. Morley, ii. 274. The timing of this project may have been influenced by the new edition of Coleridge's poetry then in progress, edited by Derwent and Sara Coleridge and to be published by Moxon in 1854.

[146] Letter to Henry Hope Reed, 13 June 1843, *Correspondence of Washington Allston*, 512–13. Wordsworth also reported in a letter to Benjamin Robert Haydon that Allston considered this 'the best engraved modern head that he had seen' (Letter of ?early Nov. 1843, *LY*, pt. 4, pp. 494–5 and n. 6). It is interesting that the original portrait of Northcote was by Abraham Wivell, who would later draw Coleridge.

would engrave another picture of his, *A Mother Watching Her Sleeping Child.*[147] Cousins, especially known for his portrait engravings after Sir Thomas Lawrence, was actually chosen after the composition of a prospectus, as shown by a printed proof copy (NPG Archive) in which the engraver's name has been filled in by hand. The prospectus includes excerpts from letters (quoted above) from Wordsworth and Allston praising the original painting, and an anonymous puff which also quoted them appeared in the New York *Literary World.*[148] A list of gentlemen agreeing to promote the undertaking included Robinson, Joseph Henry Green, Thomas Babington Macaulay, F. D. Maurice, Archdeacon Hare, and John Forster, as well as members of the Coleridge, Wordsworth, Southey, and Gillman families. Wordsworth's American editor, Professor Henry Reed, obtained subscribers, including Richard Henry Dana and Professor W. G. T. Shedd, in the United States.[149] On 13 July Robinson met with Derwent Coleridge and the publisher Edward Moxon, and concluded that 'The proposed engraving appears to be sufficiently subscribed for.'[150] Published for George T. Barnard in 1854, Cousins' superb mezzotint takes full advantage of the contrast of light and darkness (in which respect it may be compared with Say's engraving after Northcote), including a reflection of light from the subject's right eye, to create a memorable image. The painting itself, acquired by the National Portrait Gallery in 1864[151]

[147] Letter to James McMurtie, 2 Mar. 1837, *Correspondence of Washington Allston*, 399, 400 n. No such engraving is known.

[148] 'Portrait of Coleridge', *Literary World*, 356, 26 Nov. 1853, p. 281.

[149] Partial list headed 'Engraving of Allston's Portrait of S. T. Coleridge', with MS letter from Henry Reed to Derwent Coleridge, 27 Mar. 1854 (The Historical Society of Pennsylvania).

[150] *Henry Crabb Robinson*, ed. Morley, ii. 726.

[151] According to Sandford, *Thomas Poole and His Friends*, ii. 317, Josiah Wade told Poole he had left his Allston portrait to Coleridge in his will, but Wade survived Coleridge. Wade 'thought Hartley "too unsettled" to transfer the bequest to him'. She continues, 'Poole suggested Sara's name, but apparently the suggestion was not accepted'. Wordsworth, too, wanted Sara to have the picture for the term of her life, according to her own note in Henry Crabb Robinson's copy of *The Memoirs of William Wordsworth* by Christopher Wordsworth (see Broughton, *Sara Coleridge and Henry Reed*, 124). Wordsworth elsewhere expressed the hope that the painting would first go to Sara and then pass to

and currently displayed at the Wordsworth Museum, Grasmere, has deservedly become one of the best-known portraits of Coleridge.

1816–1826

The next two Coleridge portraits to be executed were drawings by Charles Robert Leslie. Leslie, whose father was an American of Scottish descent, had received his earliest art training in Pennsylvania and had been awarded £100 by the Pennsylvania Academy of Fine Arts for study in Europe.[152] Entering the Royal Academy schools in 1813, he became a frequent and extensive exhibitor at the Royal Academy from that year on. Not principally a portrait artist, he painted scenes from Shakespeare, Cervantes, and Sterne among others. He was a close friend of Allston, who probably introduced him to Coleridge, as well as of John Constable, whose biography he later wrote. Leslie's first drawing of Coleridge (Cat. no. 16) has the distinction of being the first portrait taken after Coleridge's move to Highgate. The artist himself described the circumstances in a letter to his sister Eliza dated 3 June 1816:

> Mr. Coleridge is at present here; he has just published his poem of 'Cristabel' [*sic*]. He lives at Highgate (about three miles from us) in a most delightful family. He requested me to sketch his face, which I did, out there, and by that means became acquainted with Mr. and Mrs. Gillman, who are the sort of people you become intimate with at once.[153]

The artist evidently presented this picture to the poet, for

Jesus College (letter to John Peace, 30 Aug. 1839, *LY*, pt. 3, pp. 722–30) or to the Fitzwilliam Museum, then being planned (letter to Henry Reed, 27 Mar. 1843, pt. 4, pp. 414–15).

[152] See Jane Turner (ed.), *The Dictionary of Art* (New York: Grove, 1996), xix. 239–41.

[153] Charles Robert Leslie, *Autobiographical Recollections*, ed. Tom Taylor (2 vols.; London: John Murray, 1860), 199. Leslie's portrait drawing of James Gillman is reproduced in A. W. Gillman, *The Gillmans of Highgate with Letters from Samuel Taylor Coleridge* (London: Elliot Stock, 1895), facing p. 21.

12. C. R. Leslie

according to A. W. Gillman, Leslie wrote to Coleridge 'probably in the year 1816' asking 'if you would like to have the sketch I made yesterday framed', and adding 'I shall not attempt a copy of it, in which I am almost sure of not succeeding.'[154] The drawing itself is a very informal sketch in charcoal and white, showing a rather puffy-faced Coleridge with considerable sideburns, wearing a dark coat and white cravat. As in a number of earlier portraits, the lips are parted, showing some teeth. This drawing, having passed from the poet to James Gillman and then to his widow, was seen in 1847 by Sara Coleridge, who found it 'ugly but not uninteresting'.[155] The whereabouts of the original are now unknown,[156] but a replica that belonged first to Hartley, then to Derwent, then to Ernest Hartley Coleridge, is in the Humanities Research Center of the University of Texas.[157]

Leslie executed a second, much more finished, drawing (Cat. no. 17) in 1818.[158] The circumstances were that Coleridge was ill and Leslie came to call on him with Allston, who had just been elected an ARA. Allston brought with him as a gift a portrait of Coleridge's 16-year-old daughter, Sara (whom the poet had not seen since 1812) by William Collins.[159] 'Ill and [an]xious as I was,' the poet wrote to Charlotte Brent on 4 November 1818, 'Lesly

[154] Gillman, *The Gillmans of Highgate*, 20.

[155] In the same letter to John Taylor Coleridge, 19 Oct. 1847 (Grantz, no. 828, i. 383), SC refers to 'a delightful sketch of Mr. Gillman by Leslie'.

[156] It is reproduced in Gillman, *The Gillmans of Highgate*, facing p. 16.

[157] Information about provenance from MS Note by E. H. Coleridge, 21 May 1914, affixed to the back of the picture in the Harry Ransom Center for the Humanities, University of Texas at Austin. Kathleen Coburn writes: 'On Green's death in 1845, and on Sara's in 1851, their collections went to Derwent, and in succession to his son, Ernest Hartley, then to his son the Rev. Gerard of Leatherhead, what was left after various depletions, to his son A. H. B. Coleridge, the solicitor.' *In Pursuit of Coleridge* (London: Bodley Head, 1977), 124.

[158] Although Leslie later misremembered the year, writing on the lower part of the drawing 'Mr. Coleridge sat to me for this sketch about 1824,' there is ample evidence for the earlier date.

[159] Collins's portrait had been painted at Keswick and then exhibited as *The Highland Girl* at the RA earlier that year. Leslie wrote to Allston that he showed it to Coleridge 'as one of my own, to see if he would discover the likeness, which he did' (letter, 7 Nov. 1818, quoted by Flagg, *Allston*, 143). Coleridge, who was later given the picture, called it 'the most beautiful Fancy-figure, I ever saw' (letter to Charlotte Brent, 4 Nov. 1818, *CL* iv. 878). It hung in his bed-and-book room, as can be seen in the drawing and lithograph by

Mr Coleridge
Mr Coleridge sat to me for this sketch about 182

13. C. R. Leslie

[*sic*] contrived to take a head of me which appears to be the most striking Likeness ever taken—perhaps because I did not *sit* for it. It was for him[self]'.[160] Leslie's 1818 drawing shows Coleridge with much longer hair than in 1816. His eyes are raised in the position that Coleridge had come to prefer. As E. H. Coleridge wrote in his MS Notes, 'His eyes have the look of inspiration—that beholding of the visions.' Some fifteen years later, Coleridge called this portrait 'in point of something like expression the best.'[161] This image of the poet became well known through reproductions, starting with Henry Meyer's excellent engraving, showing a gleam of light in the poet's eyes, in the *New Monthly Magazine* for 1 April 1819.[162] The 1818 drawing was also a principal source for Hamo Thornycroft's bust of Coleridge for Westminster Abbey, exhibited at the Royal Academy in 1884. A comic postscript to the Leslie portraits occurred in 1825, when Coleridge thought that Leslie, characterized in a letter to John Taylor Coleridge on 8 April 1825 as 'a pupil and friend of a very dear friend of mine, Allston', had 'introduced a portrait of me in a picture from Sir W. Scott's Antiquary as Dr Dusterwind.' Coleridge thought he was being satirized as 'A High German

George Scharf the elder. See *CL* iv. 879 n.; E. L. Griggs, *Coleridge Fille: A Biography of Sara Coleridge* (London: Oxford University Press, 1940), 32, 38; and Mudge, *Sara Coleridge*, 28, 271 n. 14). Coleridge left this painting not to SC but to Anne Gillman with his other pictures and engravings. (See E. L. Griggs, 'The Will of Coleridge', *CL* vi. 999.) SC saw these in Anne Gillman's possession in 1847, as attested by her letter to John Taylor Coleridge, 19 Oct. 1847 (Grantz, no. 828, ii. 383). Sara mentions 'a delightful sketch of Mr. Gillman by Leslie, an ugly but not uninteresting one of my Father, by the same hand, portraits of Mr. Green, myself by Collins, etc.'. The 1818 Leslie portrait had belonged to Coleridge, and the ones of Green (by Catherine de Predl, see below) and of SC hung in the poet's bed-and-book room.

[160] *CL* iv. 878–9.

[161] Letter to the engraver and publisher E. F. Finden, 6 Nov. 1833, *CL* vi. 973.

[162] Coleridge wrote to Leslie on 1 Mar. 1819: 'Mr. Colburn has entreated my influence with you to have intrusted for a week or ten days your last drawing of my phiz to have it engraved for his Magazine' (*CL* iv. 927). Henry Colburn was the publisher of the *New Monthly Magazine*. Coleridge was lecturing at this time at the Crown and Anchor, Strand; publishing the portrait may have been a puff. See Coleridge, *Letters*, ii. 695 n. Other versions were engraved by R. Cooper and James Hopwood and for William Darnton (see Catalogue).

Transcendentalist'.[163] Although E. H. Coleridge thought the resemblance 'perhaps not wholly imaginary', after examining Coleridge's own copy of *The Antiquary*, I can find nothing in common between them.[164]

Leslie's two portraits show contrastive aspects of the same face—one tending towards corpulence, the other with eyes shining. One description emphasized the first. John Dix, writing some twenty years later of his first encounter with the poet, recalled 'I saw a pale, rather heavy, phlegmatic-looking face, apparently of from fifty to sixty years' standing, with grey hairs, grey eyes, of a benign expression, yet somehow inexpressive as a whole, marked with a peculiar languor . . .'[165] When this meeting took place, Coleridge was living with the Gillmans at Highgate, and so it had to be some time after mid-April of 1815. If Dix was correctly informed that at the time Coleridge was 'in full employ upon' the *Biographia Literaria*, then it had to be during the summer of 1815, and Coleridge would have been in his forty-third year. Coleridge's premature ageing may have been responsible for Dix's mistake, or Dix may later have been misinformed about the *Biographia*. In any event, Dix's description has much in common with later ones and with later portraits.

The year of Leslie's second sketch was also the one in which the most professional of Coleridge's portraits (Cat. no. 18) was commissioned. Thomas Phillips, RA (1770–1844) was probably the best-known British portrait artist in the period between Sir Joshua Reynolds and George Richmond. Phillips had begun as an apprentice glass-painter in Birmingham. He came to London in 1790 and exhibited prolifically at the Royal Academy from 1792 on. He later became Professor of Painting there (1824), and his lectures were published in 1833. His many commissions included the only studio portrait of William Blake (exhibited

[163] *CL* v. 422.

[164] Coleridge, *Letters*, ii. 736 n. In Coleridge's 1823 edition of Scott's *Novels and Tales* (BL), the engraving in question (by C. Rolls) is the frontispiece of vol. v, pt. 2.

[165] John Dix, *Pen and Ink Sketches of Poets, Preachers, and Politicians* (London: David Bogue, 1846), 130; pp. 130–7 are devoted to Coleridge.

14. Thomas Phillips

1807, no. 274) and the famous portrayal of Byron in Albanian constume (exhibited in 1814, no. 84).[166] In December 1818 Phillips completed individual portraits of Scott, Southey, Crabbe, and Campbell.[167] With Phillips charging sixty guineas or more for a three-quarter-length 'Kit-Kat' portrait, the poet could not have afforded to pay for a portrait by him. The client, as we know from Sara Coleridge's correspondence,[168] was the poet's nephew William Hart Coleridge, Bishop of Barbados, who sat for Phillips a few years later.

Coleridge was prevented by health problems from keeping sitting appointments with Phillips in May and June 1818,[169] but by January 1819 the picture was well enough along for the poet to send comments to Joseph Henry Green, first praising Phillips's depiction of Mrs Green then in progress[170] and continuing:

> As to my own, I can form no judgement. In it's present state, the eyes appear too large, too globose—and their color must be made lighter—and I thought, that the face exclusive of the forehead was stronger, more energetic than mine seems to me when I catch it in the Glass, and therefore the Forehead and Brow less so—not in themselves, but in consequence of the proportion. But of course I can form no notion of what my face and look may be when I am animated in friendly conversation.[171]

Perhaps because of the ever-uncertain state of the poet's health, the painting was still to be completed more than two years later, when Coleridge wrote to Phillips (not without, as ever, an adverse

[166] *Royal Academy*, vi. 127–31.

[167] From the copy of Phillips's sitters book in the archives of the National Portrait Gallery.

[168] In a letter to Mrs Peter Erle, conjectured to have been written in 1851, SC refers to 'the original [Phillips portrait], which was painted for W. H. Coleridge' (Grantz, no. 1012, ii. 459). SC, in a letter to her brother Derwent, 22 Jan. 1852, mentions that 'the original [Phillips portrait] is at Salston House' (Grantz, no. 95, i. 66). Salston House (in Devon) was the bishop's; his widow continued to live there after W. H. Coleridge's death in 1849. The bishop's portrait is in the Hall of Christ Church, Oxford.

[169] See letters to Phillips, *CL* iv. 859, 866–7.

[170] It was completed in June 1819 (Phillips's sitters book, no. 479) and repainted in 1830.

[171] 16 Jan. 1819, *CL* iv. 912.

comment on his own face) to criticize a detail. As David Piper has remarked, 'Every portrait is the result of a bargain between the sitter and the artist, and only in portraiture does the artist undertake a subject that can, and often does, answer back and argue . . .'[172] In this instance what bothered Coleridge was the inclusion of his handkerchief as a prop, though to be sure he had not objected about this in Allston's painting:

It is not, I fear, within the power or scope of medical skill to throw as much Life into my crusty Stomach and its dependencies, as you have thrown into my crumby Face . . . O!—permit me to mention to you, that it is not a trick or habit of mine to hold my handkerchief in my hand—but I happened to do so in consequence of the Walk and a faintness of Stomach having thro' [thrown?] my face & forehead into a perspiration—My Snuff-box grasped in my left hand on my knee, and a book held down with my Thumb in it in the right, is my ordinary & unconscious way of sitting and talking.[173]

This feature was duly changed, and the handkerchief became a silver snuff-box held between the third and index fingers of Coleridge's right hand (though no book was introduced). An entry for 10 November 1821 in Phillips's sitters book records the completion of 'Mr. Coleridge No. 486 K.C [Kit-Cat].'

There has been some confusion about the history of this picture, partly owing to the interpretation of some comments by Coleridge in a letter to Edward Coleridge dated 19 May 1825:

I went yesterday to the Exhibition—and hastily thrid the labyrinth of the dense huddle, for the sole purpose of seeing our Bishop's Portrait—but it did not please me. It was like and not like. My own by the same Artist is very much better: tho' even in this the Smile is exaggerated. But Fanny and your Mother were in raptures with it—while they too seemed very cold in their praise of William's.[174]

[172] David Piper, *The English Face*, 2nd edn. (London: National Portrait Gallery, 1992), 249.

[173] 30 June 1821, *CL* v. 159. In Walter Crawford's view (Crawford, C9215, p. 652), Coleridge had been discussing the 1814 Allston portrait with Phillips, and is referring to it here.

[174] *CL* v. 463.

Phillips had finished the bishop's portrait in 1824, as he recorded in his sitters book. He showed the painting at the Royal Academy exhibition of the following year, where it was listed in the catalogue as no. 75, 'The Right Rev. W. H. Coleridge, D.D., Bishop of Barbadoes'. Although it has been supposed that Coleridge's own portrait was exhibited, it was not. Phillips's portrait of the poet was never exhibited at the Royal Academy, and Coleridge is comparing the exhibited picture of Bishop Coleridge with the unexhibited picture of himself. His reservation about the smile is worth further discussion, as the Phillips portrait was never a favourite with him or his family.

Phillips was known for producing convincing likenesses rather than for penetrating the psychological depths of his subjects. The Redgraves remark: 'The portraits of Phillips are marked by soberness and propriety, by negative rather than positive qualities; they are generally good as to likeness, solid and careful in execution, free from meretricious colour and truthful as to character.'[175] Phillips represents Coleridge as a genial, clubbable man, caught in the act of talking. To facilitate this he may have stimulated his sitter to adopt what he thought was a characteristic expression, as he had for William Blake. With Coleridge, however, Phillips looked for genial spirits rather than rapt poetic expression. Coleridge himself would no doubt have preferred something closer to the latter, or at least a depiction of himself with eyes upraised. When asked by E. F. Finden to recommend a portrait of himself in 1833 (see below), it was one of Leslie's drawings that he mentioned. Sara Coleridge's verdict was that Allston's 1814 portrait was superior because 'That by Phillips has his social look, but very little of his intellect. It is a gentlemanly picture.'[176] There seems no doubt, however, that it was a convincing image. The poet is shown seated against a dark background, wearing a black

[175] R. and S. Redgrave, *A Century of British Painters* (Ithaca, NY: Cornell University Press, 1981), 244.

[176] See Broughton, *Sara Coleridge and Henry Reed*, 105. However, in a letter to DC, 22 Jan. 1852, she referred to the original Phillips portrait (then at Salston House) as 'very pleasing' (Grantz, 95, i. 66).

coat and white cravat. His complexion is pinkish, his lips moist, his eyes olive-green, and his hair grey tending towards white. Thomas Dibdin wrote, 'I saw Mr. Phillips in the execution, or rather, perhaps, finishing of that portrait—and I thought it, and yet think it, abundantly resembling—'Vir ipsissimus.' Could sound have come from the lips, or action have been imparted to the eye or hands of that painted portrait, there was Coleridge Himself.'[177] We also have E. H. Coleridge's testimony that according to John Duke, Lord Coleridge (who, as we have seen, remembered his great-uncle) 'this was the best presentation of the outward man'.[178] The disagreement is not over whether Phillips's portrait is a good likeness but rather over what kind of likeness it should have been.

A replica of the original portrait, also by Phillips, was used, appropriately, as the basis of the frontispiece for the posthumously published *Table Talk*. Henry Nelson Coleridge had originally hoped to keep this picture in the Coleridge family. He wrote to John Taylor Coleridge on 17 August 1834:

I have seen the copy of S.T.C.'s portrait, & received Phillips's terms. He asks sixty guineas, twenty less than the price of the original I think it likely that he would have let it go under sixty, if an application had been made before the death. But the value is increased now, & no doubt the painter understands Horace—sublatum ex oculis quaerimus—I do not think the copy is as good as the original—& the original is the Coleridge of 40 years of age. His latter face dwells most upon my mind; but still I see that it is an excellent portrait of the man upon the whole, alltho' [*sic*] more happy in expressing the truth of manner of the outer person than the translucence of the mind I suppose Allston's portrait possessed by Mr. Wade is the fairest of all I fear 60 guñs will be too much for your prudence, as I wish very much we had the picture in the family. I almost suggest a joint purchase, if it could be managed.[179]

[177] T. Dibdin, *Reminiscences of a Literary Life* (2 vols.; London: John Major, 1836), i. 255–6 n.

[178] Coleridge, *Letters*, ii, 699 n. EHC's own view was that 'It is a mask of the man rather than the man himself' (MS Notes).

[179] BL Add. MS 47557 fos. 109–109^{v}. Of course Coleridge would have been about 47 when the original was painted. The Latin is from the *Odes*, 3. 24. 32: 'We mourn it only when snatched from sight' (*Horace: The Odes and Epodes*, trans. C. E. Bennett (Cambridge, Mass.: Harvard University Press, 1988), 254–5).

15. Thomas Phillips, replica (slightly cropped)

While his edition of the *Table Talk* was being prepared, H. N. Coleridge advised John Murray that the Phillips portrait might be reproduced as the frontispiece, for, although he considered Allston's portrait the best, for some unknown reason he did not think Josiah Wade would consent to having it reproduced. 'There are numerous other drawings of Mr C,' he continued,

—none of them satisfactory: The one most likely to serve as an average likeness—& at the same time be accessible—is the picture by Phillips—the history of [?]which you know. There is a copy also, not so good. Whether the Bp of Barbadoes [*sic*], my cousin, is to have the original or not, is at this moment uncertain.&negotiations being still pending. As far as he is concerned, you may do what you please with it.[180]

Evidently a joint purchase of the replica by the Coleridges could not be managed, and Murray became interested in acquiring the picture. In answer to an inquiry from Murray's son, Phillips wrote, 'Your father would be exceedingly welcome to the picture of Coleridge and to the picture itself if he will accept it, but I have only an unfinished Copy. The original is with the Bishop of Barbadoes.'[181] Phillips must have finished the replica before transferring it, as there is nothing that appears unfinished about the Murray version, with its very attractive flesh tones and a glimpse of red upholstery behind the sitter. Nevertheless, Sara Coleridge later found it 'very inferior to the original', which she termed 'very pleasing'.[182]

Louis Haghe, a painter, printmaker, and head of a lithographic firm, with whom John Murray had frequent dealings, was commissioned to reproduce the Phillips portraits for *Table Talk*. On a page dated 10 August 1835 an entry was made in Murray's ledger book recording the payment of £11 for 'Lithographing Portrait & study of Coleridge'. The lithograph of the study, known as Coleridge's 'bed-and-book-room', was after a much

[180] Letter, 22 Dec. 1834, John Murray Archive. As we have seen, Bishop W. H. Coleridge did obtain possession.

[181] Letter, Feb. 1835, John Murray Archive.

[182] Letters to Mrs Peter Erle, ?1851, Grantz, no. 1012, ii. 459; and to DC, 22 Jan. 1852, Grantz, no. 95, i. 66.

larger lithograph by George Scharf the elder (based on his own drawing), which H. N. Coleridge had recommended for the frontispiece of the second volume in the letter of 22 December 1834 already cited:

> Touching the 2nd volume—by much the most interesting thing would be a copy of the drawing which I send. The original is Mr Green's property & a small number only were lithographed. I will ask his leave to have it copied—but I am not very sure of obtaining it.
>
> Please to take care of the lithograph & return it to me by & by.

Almost immediately he had second thoughts about this, writing on 26 December, 'You may copy the lithograph of the Study, if it suits. But what do you say to a drawing of the beautiful church of Ottery St. Mary (Mr C's birthplace)—which I can furnish; or a likeness of him done a year or two before his death—good tho' wooden.'[183] It would be interesting to know what the 'good tho' wooden' portrait was; the known candidates would be either the Kayser or the Wivell portrait (discussed below). In the end, a second portrait was not used for volume ii. This may have been just as well, for the reproduction made of Phillips's portrait for volume i was vehemently condemned by H. N. Coleridge, who, in a letter accompanying the gift of a copy of *Table Talk* to Thomas Poole, called it 'vile'.[184] A new lithograph by Edward Finden after the Phillips portrait was substituted in the one-volume second edition (the print bears the date 1837, although the title page of the second edition is dated 1836). In the Finden version Coleridge looks even jollier and fleshier than in the first, and it is hard to believe that Coleridge's daughter and son-in-law were any the more pleased with it.

[183] John Murray Archive.

[184] Letter to Thomas Poole, 25 May 1838, John Murray Archive. SC later commented, 'The frontispiece of the Table Talk of S. T. Coleridge, an engraving from Phillips' portrait of my Father, always vexes me when I look at it. It is so much less pleasing and gentlemanly than the copy in Murray's possession . . . from which it is done' (letter to Mrs Peter Erle, ?1851, Grantz, no. 1012, ii. 459). In a letter to Derwent Coleridge, 22 Jan. 1852, she says, 'The frontispiece to the Table Talk is odious' (Grantz, no. 95, i. 66). In these letters SC seems not to distinguish between the different frontispieces of the two editions.

A conundrum exists concerning the Haghe reproduction. In the British Museum, Department of Prints and Drawings, are a lithograph and an engraving on zinc, both by Louis Haghe. The former measures $5\frac{3}{8} \times 6\frac{5}{8}$ in. and does not show Coleridge's right arm. The latter measures $3\frac{9}{16} \times 5\frac{1}{4}$ in. and does show the arm. In comparison, the tipped-in frontispiece of *Table Talk* 1835 measures $3\frac{1}{2} \times 5\frac{1}{4}$ in. and shows the right arm. The lithograph would seem too large for *Table Talk* while the zinc engraving is approximately the right size. This and the visible hand suggests that either the zinc engraving was used instead of the lithograph or that a new lithograph was made after the zinc engraving. Also, in a letter to John Murray dated 19 May 1836, Thomas Phillips apologized for the quality of a lithograph by Haghe, writing: 'He did not bring it to me at all. It is lamentably coarse and vulgar. The small one is better than this.'[185] If it were not for the date, one might think the subject was the Coleridge portrait. However, the first edition of *Table Talk* had been in print for some six months. The letter might possibly refer to another attempt by Haghe for the second edition before Finden replaced him. On the other hand, Haghe did a considerable amount of work for Murray, and some entirely different project may be involved.

These developments concerning the reproduction of the Phillips portrait occurred, of course, after Coleridge's death. To resume the story of the lifetime representations of the poet, we must go back to 1823–4, though it is not at all certain that the images of Coleridge in the two pictures at hand were actually taken from life. One, an engraving by Charles Mottram (Cat. no. 19) probably executed *c.*1823–4, shows one of the celebrated breakfast parties given by Samuel Rogers, the banker-poet. Included are a number of famous figures of the literary and art worlds, including J. M. W. Turner, Thomas Campbell, Lord Byron, Thomas Stothard, Thomas Moore, Robert Southey, William Wordsworth, and Washington Irving, with facsimiles of

[185] John Murray Archive. I am grateful to Mrs Virginia Murray for making material in the John Murray Archive available to me.

16. Charles Mottram, engraving after John Doyle

the subjects' signatures below. Rogers's art collection appears prominently in the background. Coleridge appears at the centre, but the image of him is hard to place, bearing little resemblance to other known portraits. The identity of the artist is also a puzzle, as is the date. An impression in the Victoria and Albert Museum is signed in pencil 'Charles Mottram. Artist's Proof' and dated 1815. Mottram was well known as an engraver after other artists but not as a portraitist, and as he was born in 1806 he can hardly have executed this mezzotint in 1815. David Blayney Brown has argued convincingly that the artist was John Doyle (shortly to become one of the most successful caricaturists of his time as 'H.B.'), as suggested by the contemporary pencil inscription on a proof impression (private collection) reading 'Painted by John Doyle'.[186] As Brown points out, anonymity would be entirely in keeping with Doyle's practice at this time. His hypothesis has subsequently been confirmed by his discovery of an undated advertisement of *c.*1900, in which Suckling & Co. offered for sale:

> AN INTERESTING LITERARY PICTURE
> 'SAMUEL ROGERS'S BREAKFAST TABLE.'
> A VERY FINELY EXECUTED MEZZOTINT BY CHAS. MOTTRAM FROM A PAINTING BY JOHN DOYLE.[187]

It may be that Doyle copied the individual figures after representations by other artists, imagining the gathering as taking place in 1815 in order to include Byron, who left England early the following year. This could account for the somewhat wooden quality of the subjects, who seem to pose rather than to be engaged with one another. Flaxman admires a vase on a pedestal ('carved', according to the engraved legend, 'by Sir Francis

[186] 'New Light on "H.B.": An Early Work by John Doyle', *Print Quarterly*, 2 (1985), 48–9. Walker (*RP* i. 421) suggests the engraving was 'made up *c.*1830 possibly after John Doyle'. I am indebted to Kai Kin Yung, Head of Documentation at the NPG, for further suggestions.

[187] I am grateful to Dr Brown for communicating this discovery, with other information, to me.

Chantrey, R. A.'); Byron poses in silhouette like a fashion plate; Coleridge holds a teacup. The engraving is not known to have been published; perhaps it was a private commission from Rogers.

Another made-up group portrait including Coleridge was executed in 1824 by Edward Villiers Rippingille (1798–1859), who in the period 1813–57 exhibited seventy-two pictures, forty-one of them at the Royal Academy.[188] Born at King's Lynn, Rippingille was a resident of Clifton by 1817 and was introduced by George Cumberland to many of the notable people of the Bristol area.[189] His reputation seemed made by the success of *The Post Office*, exhibited at the Royal Academy in 1819, showing 'the delivery of Letters and Newspapers at the Post Office and the various impressions on the minds who peruse them',[190] but he did not fulfil his promise. Nevertheless, *Stage Coach Travellers* (Cat. no. 20), in which Coleridge appears as one among many figures, has been called 'the most complete visual record of Bristol's literary associations'.[191] It was probably commissioned by Sir Charles Abraham Elton (1778–1852), son of the owner of Clevedon Court, Somerset (now a National Trust house, where the picture remains). A poet, classical scholar, and contributor to the *London Magazine*, Sir Charles had his own portrait painted by the Bristol artist Edward Bird and his son's by Rippingille.[192] In *Stage Coach Travellers*, a scene of travellers breakfasting at an inn, the artist has shown four of Sir Charles's daughters with well-known literary figures, at least some of whom were associated with the *London Magazine*. Southey, Charles Lamb, and William and Dorothy Wordsworth (in a black bonnet and blue dress) are among those pictured. Coleridge holds

[188] *Dict.* 234.

[189] See Francis Greenacre, *The Bristol School of Artists: Frances Danby and Painting in Bristol* (Bristol: Bristol Art Gallery, 1973), 133–6.

[190] Whitley, *Art in England 1800–1820*, 302.

[191] Greenacre, *The Bristol School of Artists*, 134. For further information about this picture I am grateful to Andrew Laing of the National Trust and to Francis Greenacre, formerly Curator of Paintings at the Bristol Art Gallery.

[192] Information from Arthur and Margaret Ann Elton, *Guide to Clevedon Court* (London: The National Trust, 1972).

17. Edward Villiers Rippingille, *Stage Coach Travellers*

out an egg in his right hand for Wordsworth to sniff, but Wordsworth's attention is directed to a watch in Coleridge's left hand. Coleridge has a fat pink face; he is jauntily dressed in a maroon jacket over a fawn waistcoat striped with blue and with blue trim. Rippingille seems to have made a speciality of this type of imaginary group portrait. In 1822 he exhibited at the Royal Academy *The Funeral Procession of W. Canynge to Radcliffe Church, Bristol in the Reign of Edward the 4th, 1474* (no. 357),[193] into which he introduced some famous figures associated with Bristol, including Sebastian Cabot, Thomas Chatterton, and Robert Southey. In *Stage Coach Travellers*, those featured are contemporaries, and it is possible that Rippingille could have sketched some or all of them on different occasions. His portrait of Southey, for example, is, according to Greenacre, known to have been in the collection of Allston's doctor and friend John King.[194] There is nothing to indicate that Rippingille ever sketched Coleridge from life, but if he did take the image from a previous portrait, which one could it have been? The previous image to which Rippingille's bears the most resemblance is that in the very rare Mottram engraving, and there may possibly be a link between the images of Coleridge in the two pictures. (An anonymous note in the National Portrait Gallery archive file says 'possibly after John Doyle'.) It may be that the decision to include Coleridge was suggested by the proximity of Clevedon Court to Clevedon Cottage, where Samuel and Sara Fricker Coleridge resided immediately after their marriage, and the egg held by Coleridge may be a joking reference to Coleridge's well-known predilection for eggs. Thomas Colley Grattan, who met Coleridge with Wordsworth in Belgium in 1828, described Coleridge's breakfast at an inn as follows:

When we sat down to breakfast, Coleridge (as usual at that meal, or with his evening tea while travelling), despatched three eggs to his

[193] See *Royal Academy*, vi. 204; Greenacre, *The Bristol School of Artists*, 133–6.

[194] Greenacre, *The Bristol School of Artists*, 135. However, Dr Greenacre believes that some of the famous subjects, including Coleridge, were probably not painted from life but from other pictures (private communication, 1996). Andrew Laing of the National Trust, who kindly provided information about the picture, shares this view.

share, dressed according to his own recipe—two minutes in boiling water, then taken out and put into a hot napkin for two minutes more, then returned to the water, but not to *boil* again for another minute—and then to be eaten. It was no small amusement to see the importance he attached to this arrangement of his cookery.[195]

In Rippingille's picture Wordsworth already has an egg, which he has been cutting, before him; and the narrative implication is that Coleridge is trying to impress him with the best way to prepare an egg, while Wordsworth is more interested in the time of their departure. Another dimension of meaning may be suggested by the egg-like shape of Coleridge's own head, as presented in this picture as well as in some others, providing a visual *double entendre*.[196]

In 1825 a life-mask of Coleridge (Cat. no. 21) was taken at Highgate by the physiognomist J. G. Spurzheim.[197] This mask was at one time well known. On 29 November 1854, while commenting on the Cousins engraving after Allston's second portrait, the London *Guardian* wrote: 'the portliness and white hair of middle life have come upon him, but the expression of his face is very refined and beautiful, and the form of his head grand and noble, and exceedingly like the well-known cast of it by Spurzheim'.[198] At first it may appear puzzling as to why Coleridge should have submitted to a very unpleasant process in which the adhesion of skin and facial hairs to the plaster could result in considerable pain. For this reason William Blake's expression was, according to his wife and friends, uncharacteristically severe in the life-mask made of his face by James S. Deville in 1823.[199] Would Coleridge have gone through this for someone whose book (*Physiognomical System of Drs. Gall and Spurzheim*,

[195] Grattan, *Beaten Paths*, ii. 120. This connection is suggested in an anonymous information card next to an engraving after this painting (see Catalogue) displayed at Coleridge Cottage.

[196] I owe the observation about the shape of Coleridge's head to Grevel Lindop.

[197] See Woodring's note, *TT* i. 184 n. 14, citing *CL* v. 460.

[198] Quoted by Flagg, *Life and Letters of Washington Allston*, 106.

[199] See the statement by George Richmond in *Blake Records*, ed. G. E. Bentley, Jr. (Oxford: Clarendon, 1969), 278. A cast of the mask is reproduced on the facing page.

18. J. G. Spurzheim, life-mask

published 1815) he had found 'below criticism'?[200] Coleridge also denigrated the *Physiognomical System* in an Notebook entry dated 3 November 1815.[201] However, in August 1817 he wrote that since expressing his previous opinion he had learned that Spurzheim's original manuscript had been botched by 'a Scotch Man' and that his view had consequently changed: 'At present I think that Spurzheim is beyond all comparison the greatest Physiognomist that has ever appeared.'[202] Various dates for Coleridge's first meeting with Spurzheim have been suggested, but whenever that may have been, it is clear that the life-mask was not made until 1825.[203] A gaffe by Spurzheim at a dinner party may have been what caused Coleridge to mellow further towards him and to agree to undergo the procedure. 'I believe the beginning of Mr. C's liking for Dr. Spurzheim', H. N. Coleridge wrote, 'was the hearty good humour with which the doctor bore the laughter of a party, in the presence of which he, unknowing of his man, denied any *Ideality*, and awarded an unusual share of *Locality*, to the majestic silver-haired head of my dear uncle and father-in-law.'[204] The approximate date of the 'phrenological examination' that ensued has now been established by the discovery and publication of a previously unknown letter that both corroborates and dates H. N. Coleridge's account.

On 11 May 1825 Coleridge wrote to his publisher, James A. Hessey, of his conversation with the phrenologist: 'He examined *my* head & found I had no Mark of Ideality—the region was flat

[200] Letter to R. Brabant, conjecturally dated Dec. 1815 (*CL* iv. 613).

[201] *CN* iii. 4269.

[202] *CN* iii. 4355. Coleridge was, however, capable of returning at least partially to his earlier evaluation. On 24 July 1830 he told his son-in-law 'Spurzheim is a good man, and I like him, but he is dense and the most ignorant German I ever knew', *TT* ii. 183.

[203] Kathleen Coburn notes that after the title *Physiognomical System* in Coleridge's Notebook entry dated 3 Nov. 1815, Anne Gillman wrote 'he came to Highgate April 18—1815' (*CN* iii. 4269 and n.); however, Coburn asserts this was an error and that Spurzheim's visit to Highgate took place in 1816. Elsewhere she places the meeting at Keswick (*CN* iii. 4355). Eric C. Walker argues that the meeting at which the phrenological examination (see below) took place was the first: see 'Reading Proof, *Aids to Reflection*, and Phrenology: A New Coleridge Letter', *European Romantic Review*, 8 (1997), 323–40.

[204] *TT* ii. 64 n.

and formless, more so than common. But he n[ever?] met with a skull in which the front[al?] Organ of *Locality* was so strongly developed.'[205] As Coleridge, having read *The Physiognomical System*, well knew, the supposed organ of ideality was the mark of a true poet. Spurzheim had written:

> The heads of great poets . . . are enlarged above the temples in an arched direction. It seems to me that in every kind of poetry the sentiments are exalted, the expressions warm, and that there must be rapture, inspiration—what is commonly called imagination or fancy. I observe, moreover, that in all persons this faculty gives a peculiar tinge to all other faculties: it makes them in every thing aspire to ideality.[206]

This is illustrated by an engraving of a domed head and bearded face much like Shakespeare's, with the organ of ideality indicated at the right temple just higher than the ear.[207] As for the organ of locality, Spurzheim defined its power as 'a facility of recollecting localities and particular places', as illustrated by an anecdote of a man who could always find again any place where he had discovered a bird's nest.[208] The dinner guests' 'hearty good humour' at hearing that the author of *The Rime of the Ancient Mariner* lacked both imagination and fancy but could infallibly find his way home produced laughter on the part of the other guests and a generous reaction on Coleridge's. A life-mask by Spurzheim was evidently the result. Ovoid in shape, wide of forehead, and broad of cheek, it very much resembles portraits of Coleridge in later life. Some confusion has resulted from E. H. Coleridge's statement that 'Dr. Spurzheim took a life-mask of Coleridge and used it as a model for a bust which originally belonged to H. N. Coleridge, and is now in the Library at Heath's Court, Ottery St. Mary.'[209] However, no such bust is known or otherwise recorded,

205 E. C. Walker, 'Reading Proof, *Aids to Reflection*, and Phrenology', 325.

206 J. G. Spurzheim, MD, *The Physiognomical System of Drs. Gall and Spurzheim*, 2nd edn. (London: Baldwin, 1815), 345–6.

207 Ibid. pl. 18, fig. 2.

208 Ibid. 364–9. The organ of locality, illustrated in pl. 14, fig. 2) is described as 'at the eyebrows, toward the mesial line of the head, a protuberance on each side which reached to the middle of the forehead' (p. 365).

209 Coleridge, *Letters*, ii. 570 n.

nor is Spurzheim known to have executed busts. On the other hand, George Dawe (see p. 52) did make a bust of Coleridge following the life-mask he had taken, and both were owned by Sir George Beaumont. Masks of Coleridge by Spurzheim (one of which may be the original and the other a cast taken from it) were owned by the Edinburgh Phrenological Society and the Boston Phrenological Society, and later passed into the collections of the University of Edinburgh's Department of Anatomy and of the Harvard University Museums (see Catalogue No. 21 and the Supplementary Note).[210]

Coleridge's health declined rapidly in the 1820s, and no portrait of him, painted or verbal, could fail to record this. S. C. Hall remembered him as he looked at his lecture at the Royal Institution, which took place on 18 May 1825: 'At the time I speak of he was growing corpulent and heavy; being seldom free from pain, he moved apparently with difficulty.' Yet we glimpse something of the poet's past self in Hall's recollection of 'the "thick waving silver hair"—the still, clear blue eye . . .'[211] Hall's description is sympathetic, but Thomas Carlyle, who first met Coleridge in 1824, found in the poet's physical desuetude an expression of moral weakness:

> Brow and head were round, and of massive weight, but the face was flabby and irresolute. The deep eyes, of a light hazel, were as full of sorrow as of inspiration; confused pain looked mildly from them, as in a kind of mild astonishment. The whole figure and air, good and amiable otherwise, might be called flabby and irresolute; expressive of weakness rather than of strength. He hung loosely on his limbs, with knees bent, and stooping attitude . . .[212]

Although Carlyle's personal animus is evident in this passage, his concrete observations match some of the details of the portraits

[210] I am grateful to Prof. M. H. Kaufman, Department of Anatomy, University of Edinburgh, for the photograph of the life-mask that appears in this book.

[211] S. C. Hall, *A Book of Memories* (London: Virtue, 1871), 43–4.

[212] T. Carlyle, *The Life of John Sterling* (New York: Charles Scribner's Sons, 1900), 54. Carlyle says Coleridge was 'towards sixty perhaps'. This description was first published in 1851.

of the last decade of Coleridge's life. The first of these, taken in 1826 (Cat. no. 22), is one that caused him considerable anxiety for other reasons. Its creator was Catherina de Predl (1790–1871), about whom little is known aside from the fact that she exhibited two pictures at the Royal Academy in that year (*The Holy Family* (no. 205) and *The Adoration of the Shepherds* (no. 208)), and from what Coleridge says in his letters. On 15 July 1826, he wrote to his son Derwent:

I wish I could afford to have a duplicate taken of a very fine Likeness in Chalk of me by Catherine de Predl (a noble Bavarian Lady by birth, tho' by the ruin of her Father during the Revolution & her own strong inclinations, now an Artist)—and I would send it to Mrs Pridham [Derwent Coleridge's mother-in-law]. Mam'selle de Predl is making or to make a Copy of this (but much enlarged) in Oil colors for Mr Aders: & another for Mr Green. Her painting is more like the best specimens of Andrea del Sarto and Fra Bartholomeo, than I have ever seen—and as to Drawing, I question whether any of our English Artists, unless it be Lawrence, that could approach to the perfect science & firm yet delicate stroke of her pencil . . . At all events, it is the best [Coleridge portrait]—& greatly preferable to Phillips's in the character & expression and at least equal in point of the Likeness.[213]

But there was a misunderstanding, and in December 1826 Coleridge wrote to Eliza Aders at length describing what had happened.[214] Coleridge had thought that Charles Aders liked the chalk drawing so much that he wished to have a copy 'on a larger scale and in oil' for which Coleridge 'was to give one or two sittings'. He hoped another copy could be made for his nephew (Henry Nelson), and James Gillman offered to pay twenty guineas for it if it pleased. But when Mrs Green was asked what she thought of the first oil portrait, 'she answered doubtingly, that Madame was still less successful in the Mouth & Lips than in the Chalk'. Coleridge and Sara called upon the painter and were shocked upon seeing the oil painting. Even though he wished to spare her feelings, Coleridge 'confessed to Madame that I would

[213] *CL* vi. 588–9. [214] Ibid. 652–3.

not give the Chalk Drawing with all it's imperfections for a dozen of the oil portraits'. But Mme de Predl believed that the portraits had been commissioned and sent a note asking for thirty pounds for two portraits. Coleridge hoped that the Aders would help him, as he could not pay for the pictures.

Although little more is known about this artist and her portraits, several points are fairly clear. Coleridge may have met Catherine de Predl through the Aders, who were an important conduit for art and artists from Germany to England. She was at the time about 36 years old, and Coleridge's eagerness to help her may have been stimulated as much by her personal charm as her artistic accomplishment. Her initial portrait was in pastel, the medium of the very striking portrait by an unknown artist in Germany drawn some twenty-eight years earlier, which may have struck a chord of remembrance in the poet. Mrs Green singled out the mouth and lips of the oil copy for criticism; as we have seen before, it was the lower part of Coleridge's face that had posed the greatest problem for some previous portraitists. If Catherine de Predl's primary medium was chalk, she may well have had difficulties in making the transition to oils. (One would like to know in what medium the portraits of others that Coleridge in his letter to Derwent calls 'admirable likenesses' were executed.) As the original pastel is, unfortunately, untraced, we can get an idea of it only through the oil copies.

At least two copies of the de Predl portrait are known to exist.[215] One (Cat. no. 22A), now believed to be in a private collection in Scotland,[216] was offered to the National Portrait Gallery in 1859 as 'painted by a German lady'. George Scharf the younger, Director of the NPG, sketched it in his Trustees sketchbook, indicating that Coleridge's coat was 'brown black' and the background 'brown grey',[217] but found it 'very weak and

[215] See Eric W. Nye, 'A Portrait of the Sage At Highgate', *Wordsworth Circle*, 13 (1982), 231–2; Crawford, 655.

[216] See *RP* i. 121.

[217] NPG Archive, XXXIV. L. 1.

poorly painted', and it was refused.[218] Another, in the Highgate Literary and Scientific Institution, was once attributed to an amateur artist named Cooper[219] on the strength of the recollections of a Highgate wine merchant, Henry Tatham. However, it should be noted that Tatham did not say that Cooper painted a Coleridge portrait, but rather that he recalled Cooper as having done portraits of Tatham's father and brother. As Cooper had also painted some other residents of Highgate, it was assumed that Coleridge must have been one of them.[220] However, it is much more likely that this picture (Cat. no. 22B) is an oil replica of the pastel by Catherine de Predl, and that it was painted by the artist herself. A sticker on the back of the painting reads: 'This Portrait of Samuel Taylor Coleridge was painted from the Life at the house of James Gillman in the Grove, Highgate—and was presented to me (his partner). Robert G. Moger, FRCS.'[221] As we know that Gillman had offered to pay Madame de Predl twenty pounds for an oil copy, there is every reason to believe that this is the one. It was one of the portraits borrowed by Hamo Thornycroft when he was planning his bust for Westminster Abbey. Robert Moger's widow offered it to the National Portrait Gallery in 1886 but it was declined and subsequently sold for three guineas to Ambrose Heal, founder of the department store, whose widow bequeathed it to the Highgate Literary and Scientific Institution in 1938. In 1973 it was restored and the present surface almost entirely repainted, according to a note in the National Portrait Gallery archive.

De Predl also executed at Coleridge's instigation[222] an oil

[218] Information from the archives of the HLSI and of the NPG; see *RP* i. 121, where this copy is said to be in Scotland.

[219] Kilmurray a: 47 lists a portrait by Abraham Cooper (1797–1868), half-length, *c.*1830, as belonging to the HLSI.

[220] Letter, 24 Jan. 1880, from Henry Tatham to Maria W. Moger; letter, 14 Dec. 1886, from Maria W. Moger to Ambrose Heal (Archives of HLSI). For her kind assistance in making the portrait and associated archival materials available to me, I am grateful to Mrs Gwynydd Gosling, Librarian of the HSLI.

[221] Robert Moger also owned William Hazlitt's portrait of Charles Lamb, which had been left to him by Gillman. Moger sold it to the NPG in 1878. See *RP* i. 303.

[222] *CL* vi. 652–3.

19. Catherina de Predl

portrait of Joseph Henry Green, which Coleridge liked enough to hang over the chimney of his bed-and-book room. George Scharf the younger remembered seeing it there when he went to see the room with his father after Coleridge's death.[223] It can be seen in the watercolour of the room by George Scharf the elder (Coleridge Cottage, Nether Stowey), as well as in the same artist's lithograph.[224] As for the oil copy of the Coleridge portrait at Highgate, it shows the poet with an even more resplendent acreage of cheek, to use De Quincey's phrase, than Allston's had in 1814. His face is luminous, gleaming in an almost unearthly way against the dark background, and his eyes have a liquid quality, with brightness reflecting from them. A shock of white hair accentuates his pallor, and his lips, as in so many other images of Coleridge, are open. It is a strange but fascinating image, yet one that must have had a degree of literal truth, for it accords well with a description of the poet in the memoirs of Charles and Mary Cowden Clarke:

> The upper part of Coleridge's face was excessively fine. His eyes were large, light grey, prominent, and of liquid brilliancy, which some eyes of fine character may be observed to possess, as if the orb itself retreated to the innermost recesses of the brain. The lower part of his face was somewhat dragged, indicating the presence of habitual pain; but his forehead was prodigious, and like a smooth slab of alabaster. A grander head than his has not been seen in the Grove at Highgate since his neighbour Lord Bacon lived there.[225]

[223] Scharf, in a note he provided for Michael Sadler's edition of the *Diary, Reminiscences, and Correspondence of Henry Crabb Robinson* (London: Macmillan, 1869), iii. 53–4.

[224] See the reproduction in my *Coleridge's Later Poetry* (Oxford: Clarendon, 1996), 62. The paintings are from left to right: 1 (above) two ladies and two gentlemen, seated; 2 (below), a seated man wearing an ecclesiastical hat; 3 (over fireplace), the portrait of Green; 4, a standing figure; 5 (far wall), four figures very like the first painting; 6, Collins's portrait of SC; 7, a half-length portrait. These were willed by Coleridge along with his other pictures and engravings to Anne Gillman. See E. L. Griggs, 'The Will of Coleridge', *CL* vi. 999. That Anne Gillman had at least some of them in 1847 is attested in SC's letter to John Taylor Coleridge, 19 Oct. 1847 (Grantz, 828, ii. 383). SC mentions 'a delightful sketch of Mr. Gillman by Leslie, an ugly but not uninteresting one of my Father, by the same hand, portraits of Mr. Green, myself by Collins, etc.' (The Leslie portrait was that of 1816, Cat. no. 16.)

[225] Charles and Mary Cowden Clarke, *Recollections of Writers* (New York: Charles Scribner's Sons, 1878), 35. The period recollected extends from 1821 to the year of the poet's death.

In its combination of literal detail with dramatic qualities, the de Predl portrait could well be regarded as a counterpart to Northcote's dramatic representation of the poet some twenty years before, and just as Northcote's picture is the last of Coleridge's youth, de Predl's marks the end of his middle years.

1832–1833

Although the de Predl portrait suggests a possible decline in its subject's physical condition when compared with Phillips's, it is hard to know whether the difference at that point lies in the sitter or in the artist's treatment of him. Certainly by 1832 Coleridge's decline in health was pronounced and was commented on by some of his visitors. One of these was Harriet Martineau, who later wrote in her autobiography: 'He was, to be sure, a very remarkable looking personage. He looked very old, with his round shoulders and drooping head, and exceedingly thin limbs. His eyes were as wonderful as they ever were ever represented to be;—light grey, extremely prominent, and actually glittering; an appearance I am told common among opium eaters.'[226] No doubt exists, however, in the portrait executed in 1832 (Cat. no. 23) by Moses Haughton (1774–1848). With this, we enter the territory of the late portraits of Coleridge, portraits in which the poet (although only 61 at the time Haughton painted him) appears as a prematurely aged man with snow-white hair. Contemporaries remark on the poet's premature ageing, and Coleridge himself lamented it in the poem 'Youth and Age,' begun in 1823 and first published in 1827:

> I see these locks in silvery slips,
> This drooping gait, this altered size . . .[227]

[226] *Harriet Martineau's Autobiography*, ed. Marcia Weston Chapman (Boston: James R. Osgood, 1877), i. 299. Martineau visited Coleridge at Highgate in 1832 or later. Like Carlyle, she found in Coleridge's features an index of moral weakness, judging him 'defective in will'. Her description first appeared in print in 1877.

[227] *CPW* i. 440. For a discussion of this poem and Coleridge's self-image in it, see my *Coleridge's Later Poetry*, 64–72.

Haughton (?1772–?1848), nephew of the enamel painter of the same name,[228] was best known as a miniature portraitist, though he also painted rustic and Biblical subjects and was an engraver as well. He was a prodigious exhibitor at the Royal Academy, showing almost every year from 1808 to 1848. Among his subjects were Henry Fuseli (whose assistant Haughton was for a time) and William Roscoe. According to George Stanley, 'One great peculiarity in his portraits was, that they never lost the characteristic resemblance of the person they represented, not after a lapse of many years.'[229] Coleridge wrote to Haughton on 12 September 1832 arranging to sit.[230] As was the case with most of his portraits, this one was not paid for by Coleridge. It was commissioned by Jonathan Green, a doctor who presided over the 'Air-baths' that the poet took twice a week 'as a *cosmetic* as well a Circulator of the Capillary Fluids' during this period.[231] This is shown by a gilded plaque at the base of the picture (now owned by Christ's Hospital) reading: 'The gift of Jonathan Green MD deceased 1864'.[232] There also exists a portrait of Coleridge sometimes known as the 'Argyll Baths portrait' (Cat. no. 23A) that E. H. Coleridge noted was 'taken at the Argyll Baths whither at this time Coleridge used to resort' and was bequeathed to his father by the widow of Joseph Henry Green.[233] Coincidence evidently accounts for these two portraits having been owned by two doctors named Green, but it would be laying too much weight on coincidence to assume that Coleridge frequented two different bath establishments, each associated with one portrait. By a diligent search of contemporary maps and trade directories Professor Walter Crawford has shown that the Argyll Baths and

[228] *DNB*, *s.v.*

[229] Bryan, *Biographical and Critical Dictionary of Painters and Engravers*, 312.

[230] *CL* vi. 925–6.

[231] Letter to Joseph Henry Green, 6 Aug. 1832, *CL* vi. 918; see also letter to HNC, 7 Aug. 1832, *CL* vi. 919–20.

[232] Information kindly supplied by N. M. Plumley, Curator, Christ's Hospital. According to Griggs (*CL* vi. 925 n.) the painting was given by Green's daughter, Mary Green, in 1864. As 1864 was the year in which Jonathan Green died, the picture may have been willed to Christ's Hospital and given by Mary Green as executrix.

[233] MS album in the Harry Ransom Center for the Humanities.

20. An unknown artist, after Moses Haughton

the baths of which Jonathan Green was proprietor were one and the same and that, furthermore, its premises on Marlborough Street were contiguous with Moses Haughton's.[234] (Notwithstanding, Coleridge did not take full advantage of this proximity, as he scheduled one of his two known sittings for a Saturday, a day when he did not go to the Baths, the other for a Tuesday, when he did.)[235] It is very likely then that the first of these portraits was painted for Jonathan Green by Moses Haughton, and the second copied from the first either by Haughton or by another artist.

The Haughton picture is remarkable for its strangely iconic character. In the luminous grey-blue eyes—were Coleridge's eyes blue, grey, hazel or brown?—gleams something of the German portrait of 1798–9, and the fresh, apparently youthful skin of its subject's face contrasts almost shockingly with his nearly white hair, as if he were a prematurely aged child. The latter aspect, though it may appear fanciful, accords very well with Leigh Hunt's description of Coleridge in 1828:

His person is of a good height, but as sluggish and solid as the other's [Charles Lamb's] is light and fragile. He has, perhaps, suffered it to look old before its time, for want of exercise. His hair, too, is quite white (though he cannot much exceed fifty); and as he generally dresses in black, and has a very tranquil demeanour, his appearance is gentlemanly, and begins to be reverend. Nevertheless, there is something invincibly young in the look of his face: it is round and fresh-coloured, with agreeable features, and an open, indolent, good-natured mouth. This boy-like expression is very becoming to one who dreams as he did when he was a child, and who passes his life apart from the rest of the world, with a book, and his flowers. His forehead is prodigious,—a great piece of placid marble; and his fine eyes, in which all the activity of his mind seems to concentrate, move under it with a sprightly ease, as if it were pastime to them to carry all that thought.[236]

[234] See Crawford, c9225, p. 656.

[235] Coleridge's usual bath-days were Tuesday and Friday, occasionally Thursday. He arranged to sit for Haughton on a Saturday and a Tuesday: *CL* vi. 918, 919–20, 925.

[236] Leigh Hunt, *Lord Byron and Some of His Contemporaries* (London: Henry Colburn, 1828), 300 (a virtually identical description appears in *The Autobiography of Leigh Hunt* (London: Smith, Elder & Co., 1850), ii. 222–3. Actually Coleridge was 55 or 56 when the first

Another, independent, description of Coleridge in 1828 also corroborates Haughton's image. Thomas Colley Grattan had seen an engraved portrait of the poet, but upon meeting Coleridge, found it was 'not a bit resembling the original'.[237] The engraving (which sounds very much like Say's mezzotint after Northcote) presented its subject as 'bloated, dark, and dogmatical in aspect . . . probably under the idea of giving a heroic air to the writer of heroic verse'. In person, Coleridge looked much different:

He was about five feet five inches in height, of a full and lazy appearance but not actually stout . . . His face was extremely handsome, its expression placid and benevolent. His mouth was particularly pleasing, and his gray eyes, neither large nor prominent, were full of intelligent softness. His hair, of which he had plenty, was entirely white. His forehead and cheeks were unfurrowed, and the latter showed a healthy bloom.[238]

These two descriptions, disagreeing only with respect to the mouth, are remarkably similar to Haughton's depiction. Haughton has closed his subject's characteristically open mouth, creating in doing so an expression of greater severity, and, while

passage was published. In a letter to HNC, 20 Feb. 1828, Coleridge professed to have laughed at 'Leigh Hunt's physiognomic Decision [*sic*] respecting my Sensuality', *CL* v. 729, but it is clear that it distressed him.

[237] Grattan, *Beaten Paths*, ii. 107. Against Grattan's recollection of the poet as 'not actually stout' we may set Leigh Hunt's of Coleridge at The Grove (to which he moved in 1823) as 'fat': *Autobiography of Leigh Hunt*, ii. 227.

[238] Grattan, *Beaten Paths*, ii. 108–9. I have elided a description of Coleridge's black clothing, quoted above in connection with the Northcote portrait. This kind of costume was evidently habitual with Coleridge. At Ramsgate in 1821 it was said that he 'looked like a Dissenting minister' (C. and M. Cowden Clarke, *Recollections of Writers*, 32). Jules Charles Young, who met Coleridge at the Aders' castle on the Rhine in July 1828, wrote: 'His general appearance would have led me to suppose him a dissenting minister. His hair was long, white, and neglected; his complexion was florid, his features were square, his eyes watery and hazy, his brow broad and massive, his build uncouth, his deportment grave and abstracted. He wore a white starchless neckcloth tied in a limp bow, and was dressed in a shabby suit of dusky black. His breeches were unbuttoned at the knee, his sturdy limbs were encased in stockings of lavender-colored worsted, his feet were thrust into well-worn slippers, much trodden down at heel': Richard Henry Stoddard (ed.), *Personal Reminiscences by Chorley, Planché, and Young* (New York: Scribner, Armstrong, 1875), 192–3.

the dramatically positioned cane imparts something of weakness (as it will again in the Maclise portrait) it also carries a suggestion of endurance. The wide brow with faint forehead lines is a very prominent feature, emphasized by the light falling on the face against a dark background.

Sara Coleridge, for reasons she did not specify, disliked this picture, referring to it in a letter to Derwent Coleridge as 'a bad one of our Father at Mr. Green's—Marlborough Street'.[239] However, the Haughton portrait impressed at least one friend who had known the poet late in life as a true image. This is attested by a poem published in *Fraser's Magazine* in 1836. John Abraham Heraud, one of the inner circle of *Fraser's*, who has been described as Coleridge's 'avowed disciple and would-be expounder',[240] published in 1836 a tribute in verse to both painting and subject:

The Last Portrait of Coleridge
(Painted by Moses Haughton)

Behold the Man! What wondrous alchymy
Did God and Nature blend in forming thee?
Thou treasury of Mind! thou gentle Seer!
Thou subtile, good, and great Philosopher!
Thou sweetest Bard, that erst did carol 'Love!'
Thou Worshipper and Worshipped of the Grove!
Thou rapt One! we behold thee 'all in all'—
So true, so well, these lineaments recall
Thy splendid brow, and lip, and eye divine!
Ah, *these were*, Coleridge, thine and *only thine*![241]

239 Letter, 20 Jan. 1836 (Grantz, no. 21, i. 39). In brackets Grantz identifies 'Green' as 'Joseph Henry', but SC's addition of 'Marlborough Street', which was Jonathan Green's address, is evidently meant to distinguish him from Joseph Henry Green, whose address (as DC probably knew) was Lincoln's Inn Fields.

240 Miriam M. H. Thrall, *Rebellious Fraser's: Nol Yorke's Magazine in the Days of Maginn, Thackeray, and Carlyle* (New York: Columbia University Press, 1934), 8.

241 *Fraser's Magazine*, 14 (1836), 179. This was not, of course, the last portrait of Coleridge, though it was the last painted portrait. Heraud is identified as the author in Haven 97 (no. 696), citing W. E. Houghton, *The Wellesley Index to Victorian Periodicals 1824–1900* (Toronto: University of Toronto Press, 1966–89).

It is interesting that in the penultimate line Heraud, possibly echoing Shakespeare's 'Of hand, of foot, of lip, of eye, of brow',[242] praises Coleridge's lip, for although there were many to praise his eye and brow, his lips had been considered by many, including himself, a problematic feature. (Another exception was J. L. Lockhart, who admired 'the unutterable dreamy luxury of his lips'.)[243] In Haughton's representation, the poet's rosy lips are closed and not, as in some early representations, thick. The picture as a whole conveys a startling sense of presence, and it is fitting that this memorable image belongs to Christ's Hospital, that matrix of Coleridge's hopes and fears.

The so-called Argyll Baths Portrait differs from Haughton's original in several respects. It is larger—approximately 981 as against approximately 735 square inches. It is also cruder. The background appears unfinished, the pupil of the left eye appears larger than the pupil of the right, and the shoulders (especially the left) have been repainted but still appear crude. The folds of Coleridge's elaborate cravat lie somewhat differently; his right thumb meets his index finger instead of being over the head of his cane, and the cane descends at a slight angle instead of perpendicularly. When E. H. Coleridge, who owned this picture, published a reproduction of it in 1895[244] he thought it represented Coleridge at the age of about 56; but since it is evidently a copy of the Haughton original, about four years must be added to this. As in the Christ's Hospital portrait, the face is very striking, although the colour of the eyes has been changed. In E. H. Coleridge's words the eyes are 'bluish gray,—the colour of the yoke of a plover's egg—not misty or dreamy but full of clear intent vision', and the complexion is 'a pale pink, like a well-

[242] William Shakespeare, sonnet 106, line 6.

[243] Quoted by Hall, *Book of Memories*, 44.

[244] Coleridge, *Letters*, ii, frontispiece. EHC thought it was 'taken by some artist of humble origin, at the Argyll Baths' and wrote that it was 'bequeathed to my father by the widow of Joseph Henry Green'. EHC could have been mistaken about the origin of the picture, as he evidently did not know the Haughton portrait. It should be noted that Joseph Henry Green had copies painted of the Shuter and the Allston portraits.

groomed and entirely healthy baby'.[245] (E. H. Coleridge also points out that the 'littleness or . . . the compactness of the nose' corresponds with Hazlitt's description of Coleridge, something that is also true of the Haughton original and of no other portrait.) The Argyll Baths version remained for many years in the Coleridge family and was publicly exhibited only once, at the Coleridge Centenary Exhibition at the Royal Albert Memorial Museum, Exeter, in 1934. There an anonymous reviewer remarked that it 'succeeded in a remarkable way in abstracting the vigour and simplicity which were never wholly swamped'.[246]

In 1833 Daniel Maclise, who had won the Royal Academy's gold medal for history painting two years earlier, went to Highgate to draw a full-length portrait sketch of Coleridge (Cat. no. 24). Maclise was contributing greatly to the success of *Fraser's Magazine* with a series of semi-caricature portraits published under the name 'Alfred Croquis', accompanying essays by William Maginn under the rubric 'Gallery of Literary Characters'. This one appeared in July 1833[247] with an article in which the poet's illnesses were the subject of a generally sympathetic account. Caricature-like but affectionate, the drawing shows a somewhat stooped Coleridge, walking with evident difficulty, aided by a cane—a detail that may by then have become associated with Coleridge's public image. This representation corresponds to Henry Crabb Robinson's remark after visiting Coleridge on 29 September 1832: 'He was horribly bent, and looked seventy years of age.'[248] The Gillmans' granddaughter, Lucy Watson, remarks that 'the rheumatism and sciatica

[245] E. H. Coleridge, MS Notes.

[246] 'Coleridge Centenary Exhibition', *The New Statesman and Nation*, NS 8 (1834), 153. The Haughton portrait was also on exhibition. See the exhibition catalogue *S. T. Coleridge*: Centenary Exhibition Organized by the University College of the South West of England: Royal Albert Memorial Museum, Exeter, July–Oct. 1934, nos. 2 and 3. This little exhibition has the distinction of having displayed more Coleridge portraits than any other: those by Dawe, Leslie (1818), and Betham were included, as were Woodman's engraving after Hancock and two examples of Say's after Northcote.

[247] *Fraser's Magazine*, 8, facing p. 65. On Coleridge's unofficial role in *Fraser's*, see Thrall, *Rebellious Fraser's*, 8 and 312 n. 4.

[248] *Henry Crabb Robinson on Books and Their Writers*, ed. Morley, i. 413.

21. Daniel Maclise

mentioned by Mr. Gillman . . . for a time drew the patient nearly double, causing that stooping gait noticeable in Maclise's full-length sketch of this date and referred to by visitors of this period'.[249] The engraved version is captioned 'S. T. Coleridge, Esq. [facsimile of signature]/ AUTHOR OF "CHRISTABEL." ' For this audience the subject was the poet Coleridge, not the philosopher, critic, or lay-sermonizer. Perhaps *Christabel* is singled out because of new interest created by the republication of that poem in the *Poetical Works* of 1828 and 1829; at any rate, Maginn's short essay ends by wishing for the successful conclusion of 'Christabel'.

Maginn's prose sketch begins with a quotation from Wordsworth's 'Stanzas written in my Pocket-Copy of Thomson's "Castle of Indolence" ', referring to Coleridge as ' "The noticeable man with large grey eyes" '. It is interesting that this verse description, written in 1802, was still applicable to its subject over thirty years later, and the whole stanza from which it comes is worth quoting, as it includes features to be found in a number of Coleridge portraits:

> With him there often walked in friendly guise,
> Or lay upon the moss by brook or tree,
> A noticeable Man with large grey eyes,
> And a pale face that seemed undoubtedly
> As if a blooming face it ought to be;
> Heavy his low-hung lip did oft appear,
> Deprest by weight of musing Phantasy;
> Profound his forehead was, though not severe;
> Yet some did think that he had little business here.[250]

It is also worth noting that in the manuscript version of the poem the seventh line read 'A face divine of heaven-born ideotcy'.[251] Evidently Wordsworth considered the last word too awkward or

[249] L. Watson, *Coleridge At Highgate* (London: Longmans, Green, 1925), 149.

[250] From 'Stanzas written in my Pocket-Copy of Thomson's "Castle of Indolence" ', *The Poetical Works of William Wordsworth*, ed. E. de Selincourt, 2nd edn. (Oxford: Clarendon, 1952), ii. 26.

[251] *Poems, in Two Volumes, and Other Poems, 1800–1807*, ed. Jared B. Curtis (Ithaca, NY: Cornell University Press, 1983), 582.

embarrassing for publication, but as we have seen, both Washington Allston and Coleridge himself employed variations of it in private communications describing Coleridge's face when he was not in animated conversation.

The engraving impressed Ralph Waldo Emerson, who had recently visited Coleridge at Highgate, later describing the poet as 'a short, thick, old man, with bright blue eyes and a fine clear complexion, leaning on his cane'.[252] When Emerson returned home from his voyage and found that he did not have the copy of *Fraser's* containing the picture, he wrote to his brother William: 'May I tax your kindness again to enquire of the Steward on board the New York whether he has found the number of Fraser's Magazine which he promised to look for. It contains a capital print of Coleridge which I should regret losing.'[253] Maclise later modified his drawing as part of a composite called *The Fraserians*, incorporating other portraits he had done for the magazine.[254] Among the other figures (in various stages of finish) are Robert Southey, Thomas Carlyle, John Galt, William Cobbett, William Godwin, Thomas Campbell, W. L. Bowles, Charles Lamb, and James Hogg. Coleridge is second from the left, seated at a table. As in the portrait drawing, his eyes are somewhat bulging, his stare is abstracted, and a cane is in his right hand. In contrast to the convivial expressions of the others, he looks downcast. The gathering is of course imaginary; Maclise simply sat the standing figure down.

Another image of the poet in old age was produced when in the autumn of 1833, a young artist, J. Kayser, visited Coleridge at Highgate and drew his portrait in pencil (Cat. no. 25). Until

[252] R. W. Emerson, *English Traits* (London: Routledge, 1856), 5. The visit took place on 5 Aug. 1833.

[253] Letter, 11 Oct. 1833, *The Letters of Ralph Waldo Emerson*, ed. Ralph L. Rusk (New York: Columbia University Press, 1939), i. 397. See Kenneth Walter Cameron, 'Emerson's "Capital Print" of Coleridge', *Emerson Society Quarterly*, 2 (1956), 8–9.

[254] The engraving appeared in *Fraser's*, 11 (Jan. 1835), double spread preceding p. 1. The engraver was Maclise himself, according to F. O'Donaghue (ed.), *Catalogue of Engraved British Portraits in the British Museum* (London: British Museum, 1908–25). For a discussion of the figures represented, see Thrall, *Rebellious Fraser's*, 16–17.

22. J. Kayser

recently nothing appeared to be known about Kayser, owing to the fact that the poet thought Kayser was German and addressed him as 'Kayser of Kayserwerth [Kaserwerth]'.[255] However, as J. C. C. Mays has suggested to me, Kayser must be the *Belgian* artist recorded as J. Kayser (1813–53). Perhaps they conversed in German and a mistake was made owing to Coleridge's German, Kayser's English, or both. According to Thieme-Becker, J. Kayser 'led a wandering life and drew portraits of contemporaries in pencil and chalk; planned the publication of a portfolio of pictures of renowned contemporaries, which however never was realized'.[256] Christian Kramm, the nineteenth-century compiler of a biographical dictionary of Dutch and Flemish artists, records that Kayser 'was always travelling from place to place in order to draw portraits in crayon, but mostly in pencil and chalk, which were often well received and were fashionable'.[257] However, as Kramm represents him, Kayser was undone by his feelings of superiority and contempt for his clients. In 1847 he was in Holland drawing portraits for his ambitious project, and he advertised in the newspapers:

Kayser's Portrait Gallery—Kayser can tell in fifteen languages—about the miracles—his artistic pen has performed—Kayser can explain in fifteen tongues—the follies of others—But it is the others—(both stupid and intelligent)—who stipulate the amount—And it is his artistic worth that speaks still more boldly—from the portraits of this great series of men.

[255] See letter to E. F. Finden, 6 Nov. 1833, where the reference is to 'a young German Artist' (*CL* vi. 974) and Coleridge's poem discussed below.

[256] Hans Vollmer (ed.), *Allgemeines Lexicon der Bildenden Kuenstler* (Thieme-Becker) (Leipzig: E. A. Seeman, 1927), xx. 43–4: 'A portrait sketch of Dr. F. P. A. Heerkens is in the Zwolle [Netherlands] Museum; a portrait sketch of J. E. J. van den Berg was in the exhibition of artists of The Hague, The Hague, 1913. Many small, very well and finely drawn pictures from Kayser's hand, dated between 1835 and 1842, are in Dutch private collections. After his drawings J. P. Lange engraved pictures of Professor J. Baart de la Faille and of Professor A. A. Sebastian, C. Bentinck lithographed a picture of the poet H. Tollens, J. P. Berghaus lithographed a picture of the surgeon A. Nortier, and Kayser himself lithographed pictures of former Buergermaster of Groningen J. W. H. Siccema and of his wife.'

[257] C. Kramm, *De Leven en Werken der Hollandische en Vlamsche Kunstchilders, Beeldhouwers, Graveeurs, en Bouwmeesters*... (Amsterdam, 1859), iii. 841. I am grateful to Ingrid Amiri for this translation from the Dutch.

In Utrecht, Kramm relates, 'some [sitters] walked out because of his disrespectful way of speaking and his ridiculing of others'. Later, news arrived from Dusseldorf that the project was cancelled, and Kayser offered the portraits he had drawn at greatly reduced prices. He is reported to have died in 1853, aged 40.

Kayser was hardly a commercial success and his overconfident, caustic manner may have been largely responsible for this. Yet we can imagine him at the age of 19 or 20 impressing Coleridge with his jaunty self-confidence. Coleridge evidently liked his young visitor and addressed a poem to him.

To the Young Artist
Kayser of Kayserwerth

Kayser! to whom, as to a second self,
Nature, or Nature's next-of-kin, the Elf,
Hight Genius, hath dispensed the happy skill
To cheer or soothe the parting friend's 'Alas!'
Turning the blank scroll to a magic glass,
That makes the absent present at our will;
And to the shadowing of thy pencil gives
Such seeming substance, that it almost lives

Well hast thou given the thoughtful Poet's face!
Yet hast thou on the tablet of his mind
A more delightful portrait left behind—
Even thy own youthful beauty, and artless grace,
Thy natural kindness and eyes bright with glee!
Kayser! farewell!
Be wise! be happy! and forget not me.[258]

This poem is a modified sonnet, one of several written in Coleridge's later years,[259] this one rhyming aabccbddeffe[x]e. It invokes the ideal of the portrait—making the absent present for the benefit of the parting friend, and suggests that Kayser has been successful in giving an illusory substance to his artistic image. This involves a play on words in which 'shadowing of thy

[258] *CPW* i. 490; first published in the *Poetical Works* of 1834.
[259] See my *Coleridge's Later Poetry*, 70–2, 79.

pencil' suggests both the making of the sitter's semblance and the shading-in of a dark area. The poem then turns in line 10 to gracefully compliment the artist, and ends with the kind of expostulation that might have concluded one of the short poems Coleridge enjoyed writing in the albums of acquaintances. 'Be wise! be happy!' may in this instance be more than conventional, however; Coleridge may have sensed that the self-confident banter that was appealing in an attractive youth might not be so in a mature adult.

Much as he evidently liked the artist, Coleridge did not really like the portrait, or he allowed his friends to persuade him that he didn't. He wrote to E. F. Finden on 6 November 1833 that it had been 'done very recently', and he described it as 'a Likeness, certainly; but with such unhappy Density of the Nose & ideotic Drooping of the Lip, with a certain pervading *Wooden[n]ess* of the whole Countenance, that it has not been thought Guilty of any great Flattery by Mr Coleridge's Friends'.[260] The problem, as so often with Coleridge's portraits, lay at least partly in the lower part of the face, and perhaps especially in the slightly opened mouth. Also, Kayser had not attempted to idealize his subject and had given his sitter no 'poetic' attributes. The picture shows Coleridge as a tired, wan, even frightened-looking old man; it may simply have been too accurate. In the letter to Finden, Coleridge might well have been talking of this picture, although in context the reference is to another, unspecified one: 'A Friend of S. T. Coleridge's wrote under a portrait of him—"A glow-worm with a pin struck thro' it, as seen in broad day-light." '

One might assume that Kayser made this drawing spontaneously, but this may not have been the case. Coleridge told Finden that the picture was 'at Highgate', and so he had possession of it, but it may have been paid for by Joseph Henry Green. Otherwise it is hard to account for its provenance. As we have seen, the poet left Anne Gillman his pictures, but as this one was later bequeathed by Green's widow to Derwent Coleridge, Green must have owned it, at least after the poet's death.

[260] *CL* vi. 973–4.

Probably the last life portrait of Coleridge was drawn by Abraham Wivell (1786–1849), an artist who occasionally exhibited portraits at the Royal Academy and elsewhere and who had previously been known for his sketches, among many others, of the Cato Street conspirators and of figures associated with the trial of Queen Caroline.[261] It was Wivell who had drawn the head of James Northcote so admired in its engraved form by Washington Allston. Wivell's portrait of Coleridge was executed for the engraver and publisher E. F. Finden. 'Mr. Finden,' wrote Charles Lamb late in October 1833, 'an artist of some celebrity is desirous of publishing an engraving of you as he has done of Southey—Can you lend him your head?'[262] On 6 November 1833 Coleridge wrote to Finden mentioning the Kayser drawing but recommending Leslie's portrait of 1818.[263] However, Finden evidently decided to commission a new portrait by Wivell. Coleridge jotted into a Notebook 'Wavill[?] Portrait Painter', with the address '35, Edward Street/ Hampstead Road,' and although this address may have been out of date, Coleridge evidently found Wivell's studio.[264] After the portrait was executed it was engraved by W. Wagstaff. Some confusion has been caused by the fact that Finden himself executed the frontispiece (after Phillips) for the second edition of *Table Talk*, but that was an entirely different project. It has also been reported erroneously that the Wivell portrait was executed for Thomas Moore's *Life of Byron*, published by John Murray in 1833,[265] but although an example of Wagstaff's engraving was tipped into at least one

[261] See Paley, *Coleridge's Later Poetry*, 132–3. Wivell exhibited at the RA in 1822, 1830, 1850, 1851, 1852, 1853, and 1854: *Royal Academy*, viii. 327; *Dict.* 308.

[262] E. V. Lucas (ed.), *The Letters of Charles Lamb* (London: J. M. Dent and Methuen, 1935), iii. 389.

[263] *CL* vi. 973–4.

[264] Notebook Q, Berg Collection, NYPL fo. 77. The entry is undated but could not have been made before July 1833, when Coleridge acquired the notebook. I am grateful to Anthony Harding and Mary Anne Perkins for this information. Although Wivell's address was indeed given as 5 Edward Street, Hampstead Road, in the RA exhibition catalogue for 1822, in the 1830 RA catalogue it was 135 High Street, Camden Town.

[265] Freeman O'Donaghue, *Catalogue of Engraved British Portraits in the British Museum* (1908), i. 465; E. Kilmurray, *Dictionary of British Portraiture* (London: Batsford, 1979), ii. 47.

S. T. Coleridge

23. W. Wagstaff, engraving after Abraham Wivell

extra-illustrated copy of Moore's *Life* (John Murray Collection), that is not the case. The Wivell/Wagstaff portrait (Cat. no. 26) was published in *Finden's Illustrations of the Life and Works of Lord Byron*,[266] brought out by John Murray in 1834, preceding a short article entitled 'S. T. Coleridge' by W. Brockedon. Proofs of the engraving were available early enough for Coleridge to make presents of them (one later hung in Derwent Coleridge's dressing-room).[267] In letters to Henry Nelson Coleridge and to Eliza Aders, the poet joked about his appearance by pretending to translate a line from Ovid beginning 'In truth he's no beauty'.[268] Although this could be taken as a criticism of the portrait,[269] it is consistent with his dislike of his face that Coleridge, as we have seen, expressed elsewhere; and indeed it is hard at times to distinguish between Coleridge's dissatisfaction with his appearance and with the representations of it.

[266] iii, unpaginated.

[267] EHC, MS Notes. EHC recalls that DC took him as a child to visit Thomas Babington Macaulay, and that 'I said aloud as we left there <?> Is he not like your father?' Forty years later he was again struck by the resemblance to Macaulay of the Wivell proof.

[268] *CL* vi. 768–9, conjecturally dated by Griggs as some time in Nov. 1833. The letter to HNC has not survived but is mentioned by Coleridge here.

[269] See *RP* i. 122.

3
After-Images: Posthumous Portraits of Coleridge

Sculpture

It is frequently the case in our culture that the most important posthumous representations are three-dimensional, and this is certainly true of those of Coleridge, beginning with his death-mask or masks and culminating in the commemorative bust sculpted by Hamo Thornycroft for Westminster Abbey. 'Two casts were taken of S. T. C.'s head after death,' wrote Henry Nelson Coleridge to John Taylor Coleridge on 7 August 1834.[1] This was unusual, as the normal practice was to take a single mask and then make casts from it. James Gillman supervised the making of the masks,[2] and one of them eventually appeared in the collection of the Edinburgh Phrenological Society, which may already have owned the life-mask taken by Spurzheim. That mask is now in the Henderson Trust Collection, University of Edinburgh. Another death-mask, now in the Princeton University Library, has a curious history. The mask was acquired in the late 1870s by Laurence Hutton, a collector who also claimed ownership of Abraham Lincoln's death-mask and a cast of Sir Walter Scott's, among others. Hutton told of finding the Coleridge death-mask 'in the shop of a dealer in plaster casts . . . in the Gray's Inn Road, London'.[3] There was no provenance, but according to Hutton it looked like 'all the contemporary engravings

[1] BL Add. MS 47.557, fo. 106.

[2] S. T. Coleridge, *Letters*, ed. E. H. Coleridge (2 vols.; London: Heinemann, 1895), ii. 570 n.

[3] Laurence Hutton, *Talks in a Library*, ed. Isabel Moore (New York: G. P. Putnam's Sons, 1905), 159–61. The mask is reproduced in Hutton, 'A Collection of Death Masks',

24. Death-mask

of the man, in his old age, to which I have had access'. These could, however, be only two in number: those after Wivell and after Maclise. Hutton communicated with Ernest Hartley Coleridge, whom he had not yet met, and who told him there was a death-mask by Spurzheim, but Hutton pointed out that Coleridge had survived Spurzheim by some two years. George Scharf of the National Portrait Gallery identified the mask as Coleridge's from a photograph, with the comment: 'It's old Sam Coleridge! Look at his ears! They are out of place. The ears of the Coleridges have for several generations been an inch too high.' On meeting E. H. Coleridge for the first time, Hutton recognized him by his resemblance to the death-mask. E. H. Coleridge said that upon seeing a photo of it, his wife had been 'absolutely shocked at the startling likeness between the quick and the dead'.[4] He later recorded the mask as authentic: 'the

Harper's New Monthly Magazine, 85 (1892), 783; Ernest Benkard, *Undying Faces* (London: Hogarth, 1929), 59; and in Anon., 'How Great Men Really Looked,' *Life*, 22 Dec. 1952, p. 74.

[4] 'Collection of Death Masks', 783; *Talks in a Library*, 159–61. Another cast of the Gillman death-mask is recorded as in the collection of the Warren Anatomical Museum, Harvard University. See Supplementary Note A.

glorious forehead is there, but the look has passed away'.[5] (It must, however, be remembered that neither E. H. Coleridge nor his wife had ever seen the poet.) Despite the lack of provenance, the role of coincidence, and the anecdotal nature of some of the evidence, the Hutton mask does appear to be that of Coleridge. A photograph kindly provided by the Princeton University Library shows it to be nearly identical with the death-mask at Edinburgh, and the same features can be seen in these as in the life-mask, but with the mouth turned downwards, especially at the left side, in pain.

A portrait bust, by an unknown sculptor, was made after one of the death-masks, the whereabouts of which are no longer known. It was in the possession of A. W. Gillman in 1895 and was reproduced by him as 'from a Cast taken after death, by the direction of James Gillman, Surgeon'.[6] However, the reproduced bust shows a man of about 30 with a full head of hair, and has no resemblance to Coleridge's death-mask. There is, however, some similarity between this reproduction and the first posthumous representation of Coleridge to be exhibited, a bust by Sebastian Arnald. Arnald's sculpture may, as Walker suggests, have been 'possibly concocted from the death mask',[7] but Arnald (b. 1806) could have met Coleridge, as the sculptor was a disciple of Edward Irving, and Irving and Coleridge were friends. Arnald won the Royal Academy's gold medal in 1831 for *The Massacre of the Innocents* (exhib. 1832, no. 1138), and among his other works were both portraits (including a bust of Irving shown at the RA in 1831, no. 1204) and apocalyptic subjects such as *War in Heaven* (exhib. RA in 1831, no. 1138) and *Design from Revelations* (exhibited at the Birmingham Society of Artists in 1831).[8] He showed his

[5] E. H. Coleridge, MS Notes. See also S. T. Coleridge, *Letters*, ii. 570 n.

[6] A. W. Gillman, *The Gillmans of Highgate* (London: Elliot Stock, 1895), facing p. 13 and List of Illustrations. 'Cast' would not normally refer to an original death mask, but 'a Cast taken after death' might.

[7] *RP* i. 122.

[8] See *Royal Academy*, i. 66; and Robert Gunnis, *Dictionary of British Sculptors 1660–1851* (London: Odhams, 1968), 20. The reference to the bust of Irving is printed as 'Bust of Rev. E. Irvine'.

bust of Coleridge at the Royal Academy in 1836 (no. 1119), and it was praised by *The Times* for its 'unaffected' quality.[9] Although the original has not been located, there is at least one cast, now in a private collection. The image rendered by Arnald is highly idealized, with the poet imagined to be perhaps in his mid-forties with abundant, wavy hair, an aquiline nose, wide brow, and lips that are somewhat thick but not unpleasantly so. On the base is the legend: S W ARNALD AS THE ACT DIRECTS 1835[6?]. 'The Act' is the so-called Garrard's Act of 1798, passed to provide copyright to works in plaster, stipulating that 'every person who shall make any Work as aforesaid shall cause his or her Name to be put thereon, with the Date of Publication, before the same shall be published and exposed for sale'.[10] The use of such an inscription suggests that Arnald hoped to circulate more copies of his bust of Coleridge, although no such copies have been located.

Although no other examples of Arnald's bust are known, his image of Coleridge did achieve currency in two other forms. In 1838 an engraved reproduction of a medallion after it was published in *The Authors of England*, with Illustrative Notices by Henry F. Chorley.[11] The engraving is of a profile of the bust in an elaborate frame set in an oval space. The signature 'E. W. Wyon' appears in the portrait area, and a caption below reads: 'Engraved by A. Collas's Patent Process'. E. W. Wyon (1811–85), who exhibited regularly at the Royal Academy from 1831 to 1876, was a son of the elder Thomas Wyon (1767–1830), Chief Engraver of His Majesty's Seals, and younger brother of Thomas Wyon (1792–1817), Chief Engraver at the Royal Mint.[12] He showed busts of Southey and Wordsworth (but evidently not

[9] 13 May 1836, p. 6.

[10] See T. Clifford, 'The Plaster Shops of the Rococo and Neoclassical era in Britain', *Journal of the History of Collections*, 4 (1992), 6. The petitioners for the Act were led by the sculptor George Garrard. Sebastian Arnald showed a bust of Garrard at the RA in 1828 (Gunnis, *Dictionary of British Sculptors*, 20).

[11] Henry F. Chorley, *The Authors of England* (London: Charles Tilt, 1838), facing p. 37. The text on Coleridge occupies pp. 37–43. Other portraits include Scott, Byron, Southey, Lamb, Shelley, and Wordsworth.

[12] Information about the Wyon family from the BM exhibition 'Commemorating the Nineteenth Century: Coins and Medals by the Wyon Family', 7 Mar.–8 Sept. 1996.

Coleridge) at the Royal Academy in 1836.[13] Presumably Wyon made a relief copy (untraced) of the Arnald portrait for reproduction. The engraving in *The Authors of England* was described as one employing the Collas process, which was a mechanical method of reproducing facsimiles of medals using a machine called the *Tour à guillocher*, a pantographic device that translated a relief image into a series of lines.[14] The result has what has been described as 'a lifelike appearance of relief on the page'.[15]

One other bust of Coleridge was seen at the Royal Academy after Arnald's and before Thornycroft's. This was *The Late S. T. Coleridge, Esq.* by Felix Martin Miller (b. 1820), exhibited in 1862 (no. 1108). Miller showed frequently at the Royal Academy from 1842 to 1880, often more than one item a year. On the whole, he did not do portrait busts, being better known for Shakespearean and other poetic subjects, including an *Ariel*, no fewer than three versions of *Emily and the White Doe of Rylstone*, and the bas-reliefs *Titania* and *Lycidas*, the last two seen at the Great Exhibition of 1851. An exception is *Rev. Dr. Livingstone, the explorer of South Africa; bust*, no. 1329 in 1857. 'It is his evil fortune to obtain much praise with little success or recompense,' wrote the *Art Journal* in 1874.[16] His portrait of Coleridge seems to have disappeared without a trace.

In 1875 an imaginary depiction of Coleridge as a child appeared as part of the 'blue-coat boys' memorial' at Christ's Hospital, a small bronze (under 2 ft. high). The sculptor was the well-known Thomas Woolner (1825–92), a member of the Pre-Raphaelite Brotherhood. Some twenty-five years earlier (1850–1), Woolner had executed a very fine sculpture showing Wordsworth seated (Wordsworth Museum, Grasmere), a cloak wrapped around him, and grasping a sprig of leaves. The Christ's Hospital sculpture is also a delicate piece of work,

[13] See Gunnis, *Dictionary of British Sculptors*, 448.

[14] Information about the Collas technique from Philip Atwood, BM Department of Coins and Medals.

[15] Geoffrey Wakeman, *Victorian Book Illustration: The Technical Revolution* (Newton Abbot: David & Charles, 1973), 31.

[16] Quoted in Gunnis, *Dictionary of British Sculptors*, 260.

25. Hamo Thornycroft, bust in Westminster Abbey

showing three boys—Coleridge, Lamb, and Thomas Fanshaw Middleton (who became Bishop of Calcutta). Lamb, at the left, is the smallest figure; he rests his head on the right shoulder of Coleridge, who stands holding an open book. The memorial has been characterized as 'partly a labour of love on Woolner's part, for the sake of the Reverend George C. Bell, headmaster of Christ's Hospital at that time'.[17]

By far the best-known bust of Coleridge is the marble bust by Sir [William] Hamo Thornycroft which was placed in Westminster Abbey in 1884 after being shown at the Royal Academy (no. 1788) earlier that year. There was up to then no public statue of the poet. The monument by George Martin of Highgate (*fl.* 1827–35) in Highgate parish church did not include one. It is indeed surprising that one of England's greatest poets was not represented in the Poets' Corner up to that time, especially when one considers the importance of Coleridge in nineteenth-century Anglican thought. Could a hint of disapprobation have

[17] Amy Woolner, *Thomas Woolner, R.A.* (London: Chapman & Hall, 1917), 299.

lingered over Coleridge's drug addiction, the charges of plagiarism against him, or the fact that he had lived separated from his wife? In any event, the original impetus appears to have come from John Duke Coleridge. Lord Coleridge corresponded with A. P. Stanley, then Dean of Westminster Abbey, who wrote to him on 27 August 1879: 'No doubt there ought to be a monument of one whose influence on the poetry, philosophy, and theology of England has been almost, if not altogether, unique.'[18] Dean Stanley had been impressed from his student days by Coleridge's theological thought, and in his *Historical Memorials of Westminster Abbey*, first published in 1868, he had commented on Coleridge's absence from the Poets' Corner, remarking: 'when Queen Emma, from the Islands of the Pacific, asked in the Abbey for a Memorial of the author of the "Ancient Mariner", she asked in vain'.[19] As Coleridge had not been buried in the Abbey, Dean Stanley proposed the second Poets' Corner, 'which contains Wordsworth, Keble, Maurice, Kingsley, and, of earlier times, George Herbert and Cowper'. The Dean went on to say that the fee was £200—it went to the Chapter, not the Dean, but Dean Stanley offered to advance the money should Lord Coleridge wish it.[20] By the spring of 1883, E. H. Coleridge was in charge of arrangements, and the sculptor chosen for the commission was Hamo Thornycroft (1850–1925). Thornycroft executed sculptures of many eminent figures of his time, including the later statue of Tennyson (1909) at Trinity College—justly praised by David Piper as 'impressive not only in its sheer weight and

[18] *Life and Correspondence of John Duke Lord Coleridge*, ed. E. H. Coleridge (2 vols.; London: Heinemann, 1904), ii. 279–80.

[19] Arthur Penrhyn Stanley, DD, late Dean of Westminster, *Historical Memorials of Westminster Abbey*, 5th edn. (London: John Murray, 1882), 282.

[20] *Life and Correspondence of John Duke Lord Coleridge*, ii. 279–80. The rules required that the Dean's permission be obtained and a site selected by him, after which (for a bust) a fee of £200 had to be paid to the Receiver General. The Clerk of the Works was entitled to one guinea for supervision. Information from a copy of an undated 19th-c. sheet headed 'Westminster Abbey. Regulations for Admission of Memorials to the Dead', kindly provided by Miss Christine Reynolds, Assistant Keeper of Muniments, Westminster Abbey. See also Edward Carpenter (ed.), *A House of Kings: The Official History of Westminster Abbey* (New York: John Day, 1966), 249.

stature, but in dignity enlivened by some crispness of handling'.[21] On 25 April 1883 Thornycroft wrote accepting the commission.[22] The expenses were borne by an American source: on 22 May 1883 *The Times* reported that Mrs Duncan Pell of Newport, Rhode Island, was transmitting the funds as executrix of the estate of an Episcopalian divine, Dr Alexander Mercer, who had during his lifetime communicated with the Dean of Westminster about such a gift.[23] On 20 November 1883 Thornycroft sent E. H. Coleridge acknowledgement of 'the cheque received value £63 on account of the S. T. Coleridge Memorial'.[24]

Thornycroft actually was well advanced with his Coleridge bust before he received the formal commission from E. H. Coleridge. On 21 March 1883 he wrote to Robert Moger, owner of the painting now attributed to de Predl (Cat. no. 22): 'The marble bust of Coleridge will soon be finished & I hope will be well seen at the R. A. I must apologise for keeping so long the picture of the poet, which I herewith return. But [?] Ernest Coleridge wished me to see all the materials possible, for the bust, so I thought it best to retain your picture whilst the execution of the bust was going on.'[25] He also executed a bust of Coleridge for an American divine, Phillips Brooks, who later became an Episcopalian bishop. Brooks, whose thought had been influenced by the theological writings of Coleridge and of F. D. Maurice, spent fifteen months in England in 1882–3, and before returning to Boston on 22 September 1883, he commissioned a bust of Coleridge from Thornycroft. The sculpture was delivered to Brooks in Boston, and Thornycroft billed him $42.50 for it.[26] As the present location of this bust is unknown, it is impossible to

[21] D. Piper, *The Image of the Poet* (Oxford: Clarendon, 1982), 177.

[22] C. W. Ray, 'Catalogue and Index of the Letters to Ernest Hartley Coleridge', Ph.D. diss. at University of Texas at Austin, 1971, no. 1454 p. 334; no. 1440 p. 331.

[23] See C & L 133, c584.

[24] Ray, 'Catalogue', no. 1441 p. 332. Presumably the funds provided by the Mercer estate were channelled through EHC.

[25] From a photocopy in HLSA.

[26] Raymond Albright, *Focus on Infinity: A Life of Phillips Brooks* (New York: Macmillan, 1961), 266, 430 n. 9. Albright cites 'Letter from William Hamo Thornycroft, October 28, 1885' (location of letter not given).

consider its relation to the Westminster Abbey statue. From the difference between this price and the sum paid by E. H. Coleridge, one might infer that the Brooks sculpture was considerably smaller than the one for Westminster Abbey. However, Brooks too might have made a preliminary payment. (Thornycroft sent E. H. Coleridge what was presumably his final bill, and subsequently a receipt, in June 1885).[27] A full-sized plaster model, now in Coleridge Cottage at Nether Stowey, for the Westminster Abbey bust was also executed, and on 10 March 1885 Thornycroft wrote to E. H. Coleridge about sending him a cast of the bust.[28]

The Thornycroft bust was exhibited in the Royal Academy in 1884 (no. 1788) and installed in Westminster Abbey in the following year. It was not relegated to the second Poets' Corner after all. E. H. Coleridge notes, 'The final choice of the actual site was in great measure, due to his [Lord Coleridge's] intervention and that of Matthew Arnold, Aubrey de Vere, the present Master of Trinity College, Cambridge, and Principal Shairp. When their wishes were made known, Dean Bradley no longer felt himself bound by Dean Stanley's suggestion that Coleridge's bust should be placed in the 'second Poets' Corner'.[29] This relatively small bust, bearing the simple inscription 'Samuel Taylor Coleridge', is placed high on a pillar in the Poets' Corner, in contrast to the life-sized statues of Wordsworth and of Thomas Campbell immediately below. Its features show the effect of Thornycroft's study of some of the life portraits. In addition to keeping on hand the de Predl painting, Thornycroft had asked E. H. Coleridge's permission to have the Leslie drawing photographed,[30] and we can assume that he also took the opportunity to see the 1814 Allston portrait in the National Portrait Gallery. Seen from the

[27] Ray, 'Catalogue', nos. 1457 and 1458 p. 334 (amount unspecified).

[28] Ibid. no. 1447 p. 332.

[29] *Life and Correspondence of John Duke Lord Coleridge*, ii. 279–80.

[30] On 8 Feb. 1884 (Ray, 'Catalogue', no. 1443 p. 332). EHC wrote (Coleridge, *Letters*, ii. 695 n. 2): 'Mr Hamo Thornycroft, R. A., after a careful inspection of other portraits and engravings of S. T. Coleridge, modelled the bust which now (thanks to American generosity) finds its place in the Poets Corner, mainly in accordance with this [i.e. the 1818 Leslie] sketch.'

front (whether looking upward at the bust in Westminster Abbey, or straight on at the model at the Coleridge Cottage, it has the Leslie portrait's upward-gazing look; from the side it displays the vast expanse of cheek evident in de Predl's and Allston's depictions; and it features the broad forehead remarkable in all three. Nevertheless, despite Thornycroft's conscientiousness and talent, the bust is a disappointment, with nothing memorable or characteristic about it. It may very well be that this was not the artist's fault, for Coleridge did not have a sculpturesque head. Except for the broad brow, his features were not dramatic. The expressive eyes, so important in some portraits, were unattainable in sculpture, and the opened lips revealing some teeth were certainly to be avoided. The result is smooth and bland.

The unveiling of the bust on 7 May 1885 was an event of considerable cultural-historical importance: Coleridge had at last entered the pantheon, though there was a slight suggestion of embarrassment about it. E. H. Coleridge, who had done much to arrange the event, reported that at the unveiling 'Mr. [James Russell] Lowell, Lord Houghton, Sir Frances Doyle, Dean Farrar, and Lord Coleridge addressed a large gathering of statemen, poets, and men of letters, which was held in the Chapter House, to commemorate the occasion. Robert Browning was present, but could not be induced to make a speech.'[31] Among others present, according to the *New York Times*, were 'Many members of the House of Commons, noblemen, Bishops, Deacons, and a large number of Americans'.[32] The choice of principal speaker was a fitting one, for James Russell Lowell was both a celebrated poet and the ambassador of the nation from which the bequest for the statue had come. Lowell remarked, 'I am glad to have a share in this reparation of a long injustice,' and he recalled his delight on first reading Coleridge's poems; yet he made what may have seemed a curious point in stating that he read them in

[31] *Life and Correspondence of John Duke Lord Coleridge*, ii. 279 n.

[32] 'Coleridge's Bust Unveiled/Minister Lowell Delivers a Eulogy of the Poet', 7 May 1885, 1b.

the American reprint of Galignani's edition of Coleridge, Shelley, and Keats, and that 'It was a pirated book and I trust I may be pardoned for the delight I had in it.'[33] Perhaps the suspicion that there is a subtext here could be dismissed if it were not for Lowell's conclusion as reported in the *New York Times*:

> This is neither the time nor place to speak of Coleridge's conduct to himself, his family, or the world. He left behind him a great name. Let those who are blameless cast the first stone at one who might have been better had he possessed those business faculties which make man respectable. He left us such a legacy as only genius, and genius not always, can leave. [Cheers.]

By the end of the speech, the entry of Coleridge to the Poets' Corner must have seemed less a reparation of a long injustice than an act of generous forbearance on the part of the Church of England.

Two other sculptural portraits of Coleridge deserve mention here. One is something of a mystery, its only record being an entry in E. H. Coleridge's manuscript album accompanied by a photograph. No date, no provenance nor location is given, but E. H. Coleridge, who was unclear about the date, believed it was from a life-mask.[34] The accompanying photograph shows a bust on a checkerboard table-top. Its subject appears not more than middle-aged and with a full head of hair. He is depicted in a Roman-style bust with the top of a toga-like garment visible. Unfortunately, E. H. Coleridge's handwriting is at times unreadable. The sculptor's name is given as Johann [?] Kaspar [?] Spossalerno, or Sporterno, or perhaps Sporsterno (Edmund Blunden was not the only scholar who could say of E. H. Coleridge, 'His calligraphy has sometimes incited us to a mild revolt'[35]). The location of this bust is unknown, as is the identity of the artist.

[33] 'Mr. Lowell's Address on Coleridge', *Literary World* (Boston), 16 (30 May 1885), 188c–189a. The edition was evidently the Philadelphia reprint (1831) of the 1829 *Poetical Works of Coleridge, Shelley, and Keats, Complete in One Volume*. For the elaborate engraved title page, including a cameo reproduction of the Northcote portrait, see Cat. no. 9.

[34] EHC, MS Notes.

[35] Letter in *TLS*, 14 Feb. 1935, p. 92. The first two names, relatively clear, might lead one to expect 'Spurzheim' to follow, but that is not a possible reading of the surname.

In contrast, a well-documented relief sculpture showing Coleridge in profile was placed on the outer churchyard wall of the Church of St Mary, Ottery St Mary, in 1932.[36] Its creator was the Hon. Gilbert Coleridge, the youngest son of John Duke Coleridge. He was not a professional sculptor but took up the art of sculpture late in life in order to perform this labour of love. Coleridge is shown in profile with the albatross—this sculpture's most graceful feature—flying above his head. The poet's name and dates are inscribed, with four lines of *The Rime of the Ancient Mariner* beginning 'He prayeth best who loveth best . . .' The depiction of Coleridge may bear some slight resemblance to the Arnald or the Thornycroft busts (or both), but it is for the most part imaginary, a bland idealization. Kathleen Coburn remarks, 'The bronze portrait is not very good, but the generosity of spirit behind it, and the genuine love of creative activity . . . endears it on other than artistic grounds.'[37] In 1933 Sir Arthur Quiller-Couch unveiled a copy of this plaque at Jesus College on the occasion of the centenary of Coleridge's last public appearance in Cambridge (at a meeting of the British Association).[38] There is another copy at Christ's Hospital.

Pictures

After the centenary of Coleridge's death, the urge to memorialize him in marble, bronze, or plaster appears to have become exhausted, but pictorial representations of the poet continued to be created. The results, beginning with some of the copies of the life portraits already discussed, were very mixed. As we have seen, members of the Coleridge circle were eager to obtain copies of the Shuter and Allston (1814) portraits, and John

[36] See C & L 4 c2403; *RP* i. 122 (which gives the date of the plaque as 1931); and reproduction in James Engell, *Coleridge: The Early Family Letters* (Oxford: Clarendon, 1994), facing p. 61.

[37] K. Coburn, *In Pursuit of Coleridge* (London: Bodley Head, 1977), 121–2.

[38] *Manchester Guardian*, 17 June 1933 (18d); C & L 477, c2472.

Murray was responsible for a replica of the Phillips portrait and for three different graphic versions of it. The Shuter portrait, or rather part of it, was reproduced in 1852 against Sara Coleridge's better judgement, and she also condemned the first engraved version of Allston's 1814 picture. 'That horrid fellow who published "Pen and Ink Sketches of Living Authors",' she wrote to DC on 25 January ?1852, 'decorated his vile work with a most vile print of the Al[l]ston picture'.[39] Her reference is to John Dix's series of personal reminiscences, and as Dix's recollections of Coleridge were unflattering, representing him as a self-absorbed man with 'an itch for admiration',[40] the poet's daughter was unlikely to admire Dix or his book. The unsigned 'vile print' was, Dix writes, 'now engraved for the first time',[41] preceding the Cousins mezzotint by eight years. It appears to have been engraved without much attention (perhaps without access) to the painting, giving Coleridge a dyspeptic expression and capturing nothing of the quality of the original. This engraving appears to have been the source for one by F. Croll that appeared accompanying an essay on Coleridge in *Hogg's Weekly Instructor* (NS 9) in 1852. Croll profited not at all from Cousins's fine mezzotint of 1850 but followed the 1846 engraving very closely for the features, reduced the scale to half-length, and omitted all surrounding details. The quality of the anonymous engraving after Allston published as the frontispiece to the 1870 edition of Coleridge's *Poems* is better, if uninspired. Just after the turn of the century, a reproduction based on a copy after Allston appeared as the frontispiece to Elbert Hubbard's *Little Journeys to the Homes of English Authors: Samuel Taylor Coleridge.*[42] Here the image is, if anything, more idealized than the original's, the architectural details are omitted, and the figure is cut off at half-length with what appears to be a curtain behind it. The picture is unsigned, but in the

[39] C. L. Grantz, 'Letters of Sara Coleridge: Calendar and Index to Her Manuscript Correspondence', Ph.D. Diss., Austin, Tex., 1968, no. 98, i. 68.

[40] J. Dix, *Pen and Ink Sketches of Poets, Preachers, and Politicians* (London: David Bogue, 1846), 132.

[41] Ibid. 139.

[42] (East Aurora, NY: The Roycrofters, 1900), 7/11.

previous volume of *Little Journeys* a portrait of Robert Southey in a similar style is signed 'P. Krame[r?]'.[43] More fanciful is an image based on the Allston original drawn in black chalk by Edmund J. Sullivan (1869–1933), a prolific book and newspaper illustrator from the 1890s to the 1920s. Sullivan stood Allston's seated subject up to almost full length beside an escritoire, a book in his right hand, his left hand on his hip, and wearing what can only be called a smirk.[44] As we can see, with the passage of time some artists felt at liberty to produce very free versions of the life portraits.

One fanciful depiction of Coleridge showed him as part of a group around the recently deceased Henry Crabb Robinson. Executed in 1870–1, this wall-painting was part of a series in University Hall, London (now Dr Williams's Library). The artist was Edward Armitage, RA, who had been a competitor for the intended decorations for the new Houses of Parliament, gaining one of the three first-class prizes of £300 for a cartoon representing *Caesar's First Invasion of Britain.* Robinson (1775–1867), had been a benefactor of University Hall and had left funds for the support of students there. Some of his friends thought it appropriate to memorialize him on its walls, with Robinson pictured as 'an old man writing at a table'[45] surrounded by groups of the leading figures of his age. Coleridge appeared with Mary and Charles Lamb, Southey, Wordsworth, Blake, and Flaxman. The pictures, which were about 9 ft. high, followed a method of wall-painting devised by Edward Thomas Parris. Unfortunately, the paintings deteriorated, and the walls were covered over with wallpaper. However, Armitage's pupil Herbert Johnson, who had assisted with the painting, had also made a reduced drawing that could be used as a basis for reproductions, and we have a

[43] Ibid., 7/10 (frontispiece).

[44] Measuring 21 × 14 in., it is signed with a monogram. This picture was sold at Christie's on 25 July 1972, lot 70, for £42. Photograph in NPG Archive, neg. 20489. I thank Martin Butlin for information about this picture.

[45] Walker, *Regency Portraits*, i. 416–17. Walker notes that this was painted in 1868 after a Maull and Co. photograph (now in Dr Williams's Library).

visual record of his project in the form of a series of articles by Hugh Stannus published in *The Architect* in 1887.[46]

The large fold-out illustration in which Coleridge appears[47] represents the poet in a manner that could be loosely derived from the Phillips portraits. (The image of Blake is certainly derived from the Phillips portrait of 1807, now in the National Portrait Gallery, which was well known through graphic reproductions.)[48] Coleridge is shown facing the viewer's right, leaning against the mantelpiece over which Robinson's portrait (not shown in the reproduction) would have hung, and Stannus remarked 'It was right to place the men who exercised most influence upon MR. ROBINSON's mind in positions near the space for his portrait.' From the attitudes of the Lambs and Southey, who are turned towards the seated Wordsworth, it is evident that it is Wordsworth, his right arm half raised, who is discoursing. However, Stannus, who imagined this as a gathering at the Lambs', may have been correct in suggesting that Coleridge's appearance implied that he was preparing to launch one of his famous monologues. The entire scene may be thought of as a posthumous counterpart to the appearance of Coleridge in Mottram's engraving of Samuel Rogers's breakfast party. In any representation of nineteenth-century authors and artists, Coleridge belonged in the vanguard of the age.

Some incidental depictions of Coleridge may be mentioned more as curiosities than as portraits. One of the woodcuts illustrating Hall's *A Book of Memories of Great Men and Women of the Age* (1871) is an adaptation of George Scharf the elder's depiction of the poet's bed-and-book room, entitled 'The Chamber of

[46] Hugh Stannus, 'The Vanguard of the Age', *The Architect: A Weekly Illustrated Journal of Art, Civil Engineering, and Building*, 37 (Jan.–June 1887), 9–10, 23–4, 35; 'The Armitage Frieze', 42–4.

[47] *Architect*, 14 Jan. 1887, preceding p. 23. Imprint at lower right: INK-PHOTO. SPRAGE & CO. 22 MARTINS LANE. CANNON ST. LONDON, E.C./ILLUSTRATIONS: THE VANGUARD OF THE AGE PART 2. This group occupies half of the fold-out, design area $14\frac{1}{4} \times 8\frac{7}{8}$ in.

[48] Louis Schiavonetti's engraving after Phillips appeared as the frontispiece to the editions of Robert Blair's *The Grave* published by R. H. Cromek in 1808 and by R. Ackermann in 1813.

Samuel Taylor Coleridge'.[49] Hall has introduced a perfunctory figure of the poet seated at the table near the centre of the room, his right arm supporting his head. There is a book on the floor (not in Scharf's original). Related to this is a watercolour by an unknown artist (private collection) that was shown as 'Watercolour of Samuel Taylor Coleridge sitting in his room at 3, The Grove, Highgate', at the 1934 Royal Albert Museum, Exeter, exhibition.[50] The anonymous *New Statesman* reviewer described it as showing 'the Highgate Room with the poet sitting dumpily in it'.[51] Even less consequential is a picture in *The Gillmans of Highgate and S. T. Coleridge* by Alexander W. Gillman (1895). Captioned 'The Grove, Highgate', it shows a man in black who we may imagine to be Coleridge, with a black hat and a cane, standing in a tree-shaded lane with a church steeple in the background. The artist is named in the List of Illustrations as 'Sulman' and has not been further identified. With such minor examples as these, a phase in the posthumous portraiture of Coleridge comes to an end.

After the nineteenth century, as the urge to memorialize Coleridge ebbed, most representations of the poet were produced for other reasons. One of these was caricature. Perhaps the most brilliant drawing in this category is Max Beerbohm's watercolour *Samuel Taylor Coleridge Table-Talking*, reproduced in his *The Poet's Corner* as the thirteenth of a series that includes *Walt Whitman, Inciting the Bird of Freedom to Soar* and *Lord Byron Shaking the Dust of England from His Shoes*.[52] A very round Coleridge is shown delivering a monologue, oblivious to the fact that the members of his audience, having consumed a great deal of wine as evidenced by the numerous bottles on the table, have all fallen asleep. Unre-

[49] p. 37. This picture is reproduced as the frontispiece to S. T. Coleridge, *Table Talk*, ed. Carl Woodring (Princeton: Princeton University Press, 1990), i. Scharf's lithograph is reproduced in my *Coleridge's Later Poetry* (London: Clarendon, 1996), 62. Scharf's original watercolour is at the Coleridge Cottage, Clevedon.

[50] The exhibition catalogue gives its dimensions as $3\frac{15}{16}$ high × $4\frac{1}{2}$ in. wide and refers to L. C. Watson, *Coleridge At Highgate* (London: Longmans, Green, 1925), 51.

[51] 'Coleridge Centenary Exhibition', *The New Statesman and Nation*, NS 8 (1934), 153.

[52] Max Beerbohm, *The Poets' Corner* (London: Heinemann, 1904).

lated to any known portrait, this image derives its effect from the poet's reputation as a soliloquizer rather than from visual quotation.

In contrast, the much later caricatures of Coleridge by David Levine allude to two of the life portraits. The first of these, dated (19)66, is based upon the 1814 Allston picture but with the subject's head turned almost full face with a wary glance towards the side.[53] The neck is almost non-existent, head emerging from a turtleneck-style cravat with the chin not quite visible. The left hand holds a long pipe, presumably an opium pipe, and a shaded area may suggest the fumes of opium. There is no apparent relation to the book review this design accompanied: L. C. Knights's review of *Coleridge's Philosophy of Literature* and editions of *The Rime of the Ancient Mariner* illustrated by Gustave Doré and by David Jones. Rather, the caricature stands independent of its printed context as a grotesque transformation of an idealized image of the poet. The same Allston portrait, with perhaps a suggestion of Maclise's, is the point of departure for another drawing, dated (1970).[54] This time the image has been reversed, and Coleridge has been given unkempt hair, opened lips, and a shaded (presumably red) nose—the last a typical characteristic of Levine's drawings, though not of Coleridge's physiognomy. Once more, the drawing has no particular relation to the text it accompanies, a review of the Empson-Pirie selection of Coleridge's poetry, and the same drawing was reproduced in 1971 accompanying a review of the Collected Coleridge edition of *The Friend*.[55] A third Levine caricature, dated (19)68, is based on the Hancock portrait but turned to the viewer's left.[56] The subject's hair is dishevelled, thick lips opened to show two large rabbitty teeth, nose grossly large and heavily shaded. The neck is preternaturally long, and sideburns emerge from the hair and cover part of the face. This drawing, published with L. C. Knights's review of *Coleridge* by

[53] *New York Review of Books*, 6 (26 May 1966), 12.
[54] Ibid. 20 (14 June 1973), 14.
[55] Ibid. 16 (22 Apr. 1971), 55.
[56] Ibid. 11 (19 Dec. 1968), 25.

Walter Jackson Bate, was recycled in 1972 to accompany a review of a book to which it accidentally had some thematic relevance, Norman Fruman's *The Damaged Archangel*, and it was used yet again in 1990.[57]

An exception to the general abandonment of posthumous portraits of Coleridge by serious contemporary artists is a striking aquatint by Patrick Procktor (b. 1936). Procktor's illustrations to *The Rime of the Ancient Mariner* were published both as a portfolio and as illustrations to an edition of the poem (Guillamet and Lightfoot, 1976, and Electo Editions, The Redfern Gallery).[58] Some of these prints were exhibited at the Wordsworth Museum, Grasmere, in 1997. The series is in a contemporary visual idiom but with deliberate reference to Doré, and Procktor's dark-faced *Samuel Taylor Coleridge* which takes as its point of departure the portrait by an unknown artist in Germany.

Last, the changing vogue of different Coleridge portraits may be indicated by their use on the covers and jackets of books, especially of widely circulated anthologies. As has been seen, the 1814 Allston portrait was reproduced with a number of nineteenth-century collections. More recently, a loose adaptation of Maclise has been used by Dell and a reproduction of Vandyke by Penguin Books.[59] The Jesus College version of the Northcote portrait, little known previously, was brought to a new prominence when used for the cover of a new edition of the Everyman *Poems*, edited by John Beer; and the lush replica of the German portrait supplies the cover of the Oxford World's Classics edition, edited by H. J. Jackson.[60] Although it is difficult to draw conclusions from the choices of commercial publishers, as we do not know in most cases who made the choice or for what reason, the appearance of these images on books edited by two such prominent

[57] *New York Review of Books*, 37 (6 Dec. 1990), 43–6.

[58] For bibliographical details, see Crawford, c6338, p. 395.

[59] Design by Richard Powers, *Coleridge*, Laurel Poetry Series (New York: Dell, 1959); *Coleridge: Poems and Prose*, selected by Kathleen Raine (Harmondsworth, Middlesex: Penguin, 1985).

[60] (London: J. M. Dent, 1993); (Oxford and New York: Oxford University Press, 1997).

scholars suggests that a more 'Romantic' idea of Coleridge is being suggested to the reading public. Perhaps the day of the Moses Haughton portrait, with its startling juxtaposition of baby-pink skin and white hair, and its flat, iconic quality, is yet to come.

4
Catalogue

While even brief mentions of historical importance are referenced under *Literature*, no attempt has been made to list merely passing modern references. All known lifetime engravings of Coleridge appear here, with a selection of the most important posthumous engravings after life portraits.

1. **Peter Vandyke** (1729–99)
1795.
Oil on canvas.
22 × 18 in.
London, National Portrait Gallery, no. 192.
Provenance: Joseph Cottle. Sold by his niece Elizabeth Green to the NPG.
Engravings: frontispiece by R. Woodman, 'From a Painting by Vandyke (1795) in Possession of Mr Cottle', Joseph Cottle's *Early Recollections* (London, 1837). BM Dept. of Prints and Drawings has an example lettered 'Proof' (1853–11–23–10).
Literature: Cottle, *Early Recollections*, pp. xxxi–xxxiv; *RP* i. 118. Crawford, 649.

2. **Robert Hancock** (1729 or 1730–1817)
1796.
Pencil and wash on off-white paper.
7 × 5$\frac{1}{8}$ in.
London, National Portrait Gallery, no. 452.
Painted for Joseph Cottle (Cottle says it was done with crayons and afterwards varnished). *RP* i. 118 records inscription on back probably by Cottle: 'S. T. Coleridge/by Hancock 1796'.
Provenance: Joseph Cottle; sold by his niece at Sotheby's, 1864;

Fawcett & Noseda; Lt.-Col. Francis Cunningham; sold Sotheby's 1876; sold by W. W. De la Rue to the NPG in 1877.

Exhibitions: National Portrait Exhibition, 1868; Arts Council, Wordsworth Bicentenary, Kendal and Southampton, 1970; British Museum, *Samuel Taylor Coleridge*, 1972; British Museum, *The Shadow of the Guillotine*, 1989.

Engravings: By Woodman for frontispiece to Cottle, *Early Recollections*, ii. According to Blanshard (p. 30), the portraits of Wordsworth and Coleridge in this book were engraved specifically for it (and not earlier). BM Dept. of Prints and Drawings has a very fine loose impression (1853–11–23–11), but this may have been torn out of the book.

Literature: Cottle, *Early Recollections*, i, pp. xxxi, 179; *RP* 118–19; Cyril Cook, 'A Pioneer in Porcelain Decoration', *Country Life*, 26 Jan. 1951, pp. 250–1; Cyril Cook, *The Life and Work of Robert Hancock* (London: Chapman & Hall, 1948), 10; Blanshard, *Portraits of Wordsworth*, 42–3, 141; Crawford, 649–50.

Later version: photogravure from a copy in Indian ink by N. Branwhite (BM Dept. of Prints and Drawings). Published by William George's Sons, Bristol (1891).

3. **W. Shuter** (Dates unknown)
1798.
Oil.
Size unknown.
Location unknown.

Provenance: ?Thomas Poole, R. P. King (of Buslington, in 1852), Miss A. A. King (of Wotton-under-Edge, before 1957), Mr and Mrs Cartwright.

Copies were made in 1835 for HNC, J. H. Green, and the Gillmans.

Engravings: (Posthumous) Lithograph by W. Holl, for Sara and Derwent Coleridge's edition of *Poetical Works* (London: Edward Moxon, 1852). Sheet $6\frac{3}{8} \times 4\frac{1}{2}$ in. Caption: 'S. T. Coleridge / Aet. 26'; and 'London, Edward Moxon, Dover Street, 1852'. The upper part only is reproduced (without the book), so this engraving may have been based on one of the painted copies. The same frontispiece was used for the Moxon edition of 1863. This was designated 'A New Edition' edited by Derwent and Sara Coleridge, no doubt to set it off from other editions published since Coleridge's poems had passed into the public domain. Derwent's new 'Advertisement' says nothing about this portrait or any other.

Copies or later versions by other artists:

1. Highgate Literary and Scientific Institution. Oil on panel, cut-down.
2. Friends of Coleridge, Nether Stowey. Oil on panel, cut down. Sold at Sotheby's, lot 145 in sale no. LN5449, 18 Dec. 1995. Reproduced in catalogue *English Literature and History*, p. 61, as 'English school, oil on panel, head and shoulders, in dark coat and wearing a white cravat, *c.11 × 9 inches, cleaned, in gilt frame [nineteenth century]*'.
3. Posthumous: Harry Ransom Humanities Research Center, University of Texas. Photograph with oil overlay, $8\frac{1}{8} \times 5\frac{5}{16}$ in. From the collection of E. L. Griggs. A photographer's stamp on the verso reads: 'S. Crowden Clement A.R.P.S./ The Studio/ Church Street/Wotton-Under-Edge, Glos.' This may therefore be a photograph of the original once owned by Miss King of Wotton-under-Edge, and it or another version of it may have been the basis of the reproduction in *CL* i: frontispiece.

4. **An unknown artist in Germany** (Dates unknown)
1798–9.
Pastel.
Measurements unknown.
Present location unknown.
Provenance: S. T. Coleridge, Josiah Wedgwood.
Copy: by an unknown artist. Approximately 12 × 8 in. *Provenance*: S. T. Coleridge, Thomas Poole, Thomas Ward, Ward's daughters Mary Isabella, Agnes Scott, and Kate Ward, Helen Cam,[1]

[1] Miss Helen Cam of Girton College, Cambridge, was a descendant of Thomas Ward, according to Lawrence Hanson, *The Life of S. T. Coleridge: The Early Years* (London: George Allen & Unwin, 1938), 432.

Walter H. Cam, Mrs Cam, Keble House, private collection.

Literature: *RP* 120. Wensley Pithey, 'A German Coleridge Portrait', *TLS* (1935), 76; Walter H. Cam, 'A Coleridge Portrait', *TLS* (1935), 92.

5. **John Hazlitt** (1767–1837)
1802.
Watercolour.
$4\frac{1}{4} \times 5$ in.
Present location unknown.
Provenance: Commissioned by Samuel Taylor Coleridge. Francis Wellesley coll., Gordon Graham Wordsworth.
Exhibition: Royal Academy, 1802.
Literature: *Courier*, 3 May 1802; Graves, *RA: Dictionary*, 52–3; *A Handlist of the Miniatures and Portraits in Plumbago or Pencil Belonging to Francis and Minnie Wellesley*, Foreword by Dr G. C. Williamson (Oxford, 1914), no. 1; Sotheby, Wilkinson, & Hodge, *Catalogue of the Well-Known and Valuable Collection of Plumbago, Pen and Ink, and Coloured Pencil Drawings and Miniatures . . . The Property of Francis Wellesley, Esq.* . . . 18 June 1920, and the four following days, p. 11, no. 425; Catherine Macdonald Maclean, *Born Under Saturn*: *A Biography of William Hazlitt* (London: Collins, 1943), 126.

6. **William Hazlitt** (1778–1830)
Summer 1803.
Medium unknown.
Measurements unknown.
Present location unknown.
Provenance: Samuel Taylor Coleridge.

7. **William Hazlitt** (1778–1830)
July–Oct. 1803.
Medium unknown.
Measurements unknown.

Present location unknown.
Provenance: Sir George Beaumont, the Beaumont family.
Literature: *EY* 446; Mark L. Reed, *Wordsworth: The Chronology of the Middle Years 1800–1815* (Cambridge, Mass.: Harvard University Press, 1975), 215; W. Carew Hazlitt, *Memoirs of William Hazlitt* (London: J. M. Dent, 1930), i. 103 n.; Crawford, 650.
The last dated reference to this picture at Coleorton is an NPG memorandum dated 1938 (see Ch. 2 n. 59).[2]

8. **George Dance** (1741–1825)
1804.
Pencil on paper.
$7\frac{3}{4} \times 6\frac{3}{8}$ in.
The Wordsworth Trust, Grasmere.
Signed and dated 'Geo. Dance / March 21st. 1804.'
Provenance: George Beaumont coll. Acquired by The Wordsworth Trust from the Beaumont family in 1984.
Exhibitions: *William Wordsworth and the Age of English Romanticism*, NYPL 1988; Indiana University Art Museum, 1988; Chicago Historical Society, 1988.
Literature: *RP* i. 120. *Sir George Beaumont*, Leicester Art Gallery exhib. cat. (1974), 45. J. Wordsworth, M. C. Jaye, and R. Woof, *William Wordsworth and the Age of English Romanticism* (New Brunswick: Rutgers University Press, 1987), 233 (Cat. no. 281).

9. **James Northcote, RA** (1746–1831)
1804.
Oil.

[2] Although it is stated by Crawford, 650, that the picture was known to be in the Beaumont Collection as late as 1948, the article cited (by A. C. Sewter, see under No. 9 below) is about the Northcote painting and does not mention Hazlitt. The picture is listed among Paintings and Drawings of the British School in the 1974 Leicester Museum and Art Gallery exhibition catalogue '*a painter's eye, a poet's heart*'/*Sir George Beaumont of Coleorton, Leicestershire*: 'William Hazlitt/Portrait of Samuel Taylor Coleridge, Oil' (p. 47), with the source of information given as 'Coleorton Records'. The picture was evidently not included in the exhibition and there is nothing to suggest that it was seen by the compilers of the catalogue.

$29\frac{1}{2} \times 24\frac{1}{2}$ in.
Jesus College, Cambridge.

Provenance: Sir George Beaumont, Charles J. Sawyer Ltd.

Exhibitions: RA 1804; National Portrait Exhibition, 1868; *Sir George Beaumont and His Circle*, Leicester Museum and Art Gallery, 1953.

Literature: Sale catalogue, Sotheby & Co., *Catalogue of Modern Paintings and Drawings*, 20 February 1952, 'Paintings/The Property of the Late Sir G. A. H. Beaumont, Bart.' (comprising 11 items): no. 69: 'J. Northcote. Portrait of Samuel Taylor Coleridge, half-length, wearing a black coat and white stock. $29\frac{1}{2} \times 24\frac{1}{2}$ in. Exhibited at the National Portrait Exhibition, 1868.' (The marked BL copy says it was sold to Sawyer for £50. Sawyer sold it to Jesus College that same year).

Exhibition Catalogue, *Sir George Beaumont and His Circle*, Leicester Museum and Art Gallery, 1953, no. 12. Alethea Hayter, *A Voyage in Vain: Coleridge's Journey to Malta in 1804*, pp. 15–16. Crawford, 651; *RP*, i. 120; A. C. Sewter, 'Coleridge, Beaumont, and Coleorton', *Leicester and Rutland Magazine*, 1 (Dec. 1948), 30–5; *Sir George Beaumont and His Circle*, Leicester Museums and Art Gallery, 1953, no. 12; J. W. Goodison, 'Cambridge Portraits, IV', *The Connoisseur*, 144 (1 Aug. 1959), 9 (8–13).

Engravings: 1. Mezzotint by William Say, 1805. Imprint: 'Published April 20th, 1805 by the engraver, 92 Norton Street, Mary-le-bon. Sheet $14\frac{3}{4} \times 10\frac{15}{16}$ in. (including imprint, otherwise $13\frac{1}{4}$in.). An example in BM Dept. of Prints and Drawings (1855–10–50; Coleridge C. vii. p. 4).

2. Intaglio engraving (after Say's mezzotint) by J. Thomson (1787/8–1850) for the *European Magazine*, August 1819. BM Dept. of Prints and Drawings, has a copy on a loose sheet dated 2 August 1819. Also in NYPL. Sheet $8\frac{9}{16} \times 4\frac{1}{2}$ in. Design area within ruled borders $4\frac{1}{2} \times 3\frac{7}{8}$ in.

3. A cameo-like image (presumably after Thomson or possibly Say) in the engraved frontispiece of the Galignani edition of

Poetical Works of Coleridge, Shelley, and Keats (Paris, 1829). The altarpiece-like framework with rococo-style ornamentation also has little portraits of Keats and of Shelley. Page: 8⅝ × 5¼ in. Copies in NYPL and in Berg Collection have different inscriptions: NYPL, 'Portraits engraved by G. B. Ellis' / 'Ornaments by W. H. Ellis' [.] Berg, 'Portraits engraved by J. T. Wedgwood' / 'Ornaments by Peronard' [.] J. T. Wedgwood (*c.*1783–1856) was a line engraver who 'was employed on plates from the Elgin Marbles' in 1812 and also did historical plates and portraits, including Byron and Scott (*Bryan's Dictionary of Painters and Engravers*, rev. George C. Williamson (London: George Bell & Sons, 1905), v. 349).

9A. Replica, possibly by Northcote. The Wordsworth Trust, Grasmere. *Provenance*: James Peter King-Salter (who offered it to the NPG in 1868); J. C. C. Holder; on loan to Rydal Mount, Cumbria; sold at Christie's 14 June 1986 (no. 149). Described as: 'Circle of James Northcote, R. A./ Portrait of Samuel Taylor Coleridge, bust length in a blue jacket and white stock./ 30 × 25 in. (76.2 × 63.5 cm.).' Information from Robert Woof (private correspondence) about this copy or version, including copy of a letter from John Holder (18 Sept. 1994), former owner. James Peter King-Salter, MA (1831–95) studied at Peterhouse and Trinity Hall, Cambridge, took Holy Orders, but relinquished them in 1866 and went to France and Italy to study the arts. John Holder notes that there are Salter memorials in St Mary's, Ottery, and speculates that Coleridge's father could have known the Salter family and that the portrait might have been acquired by or given to King-Salter's father, who was also a parson. (In that case the picture cannot have reached the 'friends in the North' mentioned in Coleridge's's letter of 29 March 1804.) Professor Woof suggests in correspondence that the question of which picture is primary is open, 'not least because the Dove Cottage portrait does show Coleridge in a rather unflattering guise, something that was probably justified by Coleridge's condition in 1804'.

10. **Washington Allston** (1779–1843)
1806.
Unfinished oil.
$29\frac{1}{2} \times 24\frac{5}{8}$ in.
Fogg Art Museum, Harvard University Art Museums, loan from the Washington Allston Trust.
Provenance: Allston's niece, Ruth Charlotte Dana of Boston; Richard H. Dana, H. W. L. Dana.
Exhibitions: Royal Academy, 1812; Boston Museum of Fine Arts, 1881; Detroit Institute of Arts and the Boston Museum of Fine Arts, 1947; Boston Museum of Fine Arts and Pennsylvania Academy of the Fine Arts, 1979–80; *William Wordsworth and the Age of English Romanticism*, NYPL 1987–8; Indiana University Art Museum, 1988; Chicago Historical Society, 1988.
Literature: E. P. Richardson, *Washington Allston*, 75–8, 190–1; Gerdts and Stebbins, *A Man of Genius* (Boston: Museum of Fine Arts), 50–1; *RP* i. 120; Crawford, 651.

11. **Matilda Betham** (1776–1852)
1808.
Watercolour.
$3\frac{5}{8} \times 2\frac{7}{8}$ in. to edge of frame.
Private collection.[3]
Provenance: S. T. Coleridge, Sara Coleridge, Edith Coleridge, Revd A. D. Coleridge.
Engravings: Unsigned frontispiece of *The Cabinet, a Monthly Magazine of Polite Literature*, NS 1/2 (Feb. 1809). A pedestal-like caption: 'COLERIDGE[.]' Imprint: 'Published by Matthews and Leigh, 1809'. The title-page says 'Embellished with a portrait of Samuel Taylor Coleridge, Esq.' and the engraving faces the first page of the anonymous article 'Samuel Taylor Coleridge, Esq.'. A loose sheet with this engraving is in the NYPL. Design $5\frac{9}{16} \times 3\frac{7}{8}$ in. Page size $7 \times 4\frac{1}{8}$ in. 'Published by Matthews &

[3] A photo recorded in the NPG (ref. 6867) refers to the Bristol Art Gallery, but this is not correct (as Francis Greenacre has kindly verified in correspondence).

Leigh, 1809'.[4] Also a small engraving, HRC 79.116.2., unsigned and undated, size: $4\frac{1}{8} \times 3\frac{1}{2}$ in.

Literature: Ernest Betham, *A House of Letters* (London: Jarrold & Sons, 1905) 110, 115–17, 124; *CN* iii. 4049 n., 4062 n.; *RP* i. 120; Crawford, 651–2.

12. **George Dawe, ARA** (elected R. A. 1813) 1781–1829
4 or 5 Dec. 1811 (see *CL* iii. 350–1, 386).
Plaster life-mask.
Measurements unknown.
?Harvard University, Warren Anatomical Museum.
Provenance: Sir George Beaumont, Boston Phrenological Society.
Literature: A. W. Gillman, *The Life of Samuel Taylor Coleridge* (London: W. Pickering, 1834); *A Catalogue of Phrenological Specimens Belonging to the Boston Phrenological Society* (Boston: Printed by John Ford, 1835); J. B. S. Jackson MD, *Harvard University: A Descriptive of the Warren Anatomical Museum* (Boston: A. Williams and Co., 1870), 710; *RP* i. 120; Crawford, 652.

13. **George Dawe**
1811–12.
Crayon.
Private collection.
$23 \times 16\frac{1}{2}$ in.
Provenance: S. T. Coleridge, then by inheritance through the Coleridge family including John Duke, Lord Coleridge.
Exhibition: RA 1812 (547).
Engraving: Posthumous etching by Leopold Lowenstam. Published as frontispiece to A. W. Gillman, *The Gillmans of Highgate* (London: Elliot Stock, 1895).

[4] According to Griggs, *CL* iii. 83, citing EHC's edn. of the *Letters* (1895), the plate of the *Cabinet* engraving was later used for a 'bogus or deputy portrait of Lord Cochrane prefaced as the frontispiece of a pamphlet issued during his trial in 1814' (a case memorably fictionalized in Patrick O'Brian's novel *The Reverse of the Medal*). I have been unable to find such an engraving. There is a portrait of Lord Cochrane in the *European Magazine*, 55 (Jan.–June 1809), 'Engraved by Ridley from an original drawing by Thomson', facing p. 339, but the face bears no resemblance to Coleridge's.

Literature: *Royal Academy*, ii. 272; Lord Coleridge, *The Story of a Devonshire House* (London: T. Fisher Unwin, 1905), 10, 191; *RP* i. 121; Crawford, 652.

14. **George Dawe**
1811–12.
Bust (?terracotta).
Measurements unknown.
Present location unknown.
Exhibitions: RA 1812 (no. 922); Royal Albert Memorial Museum, Exeter, 1934.

15. **Washington Allston**
Signed and dated 1814.
Oil on canvas.
$45 \times 35\frac{5}{8}$ in.
NPG (184), on loan to the Wordsworth Museum, Grasmere.
Provenance: Josiah Wade, Bristol. Mrs Josiah Wade. SC wrote to DC on 22 Dec. 1852 that the portrait was 'in the possession of Mr [George Tovey] Barnard, Huntington Villa, Clifton, near Bristol', and that 'Mrs. Barnard is the granddaughter of my Father's Friend, Josiah Wade.'[5] Sold to the National Portrait Gallery by George T. Barnard in 1864.
Exhibitions: Merchant Taylor's Hall, Bristol, 1814; National Portrait Exhibition, South Kensington, 1868; *American Artists in Europe 1800–1900*, Walker Art Gallery, Liverpool, 1976–7; *A Man of Genius: The Art of Washington Allston*, Boston and Philadelphia, 1979–80.
Literature: Sandford, *Thomas Poole and His Friends* (London and New York: Macmillan, 1888), ii. 317; W. T. Whitley, *Art in England 1800–1820* (Cambridge: Cambridge University Press, 1928), 236; *RP* i. 119–20; E. P. Richardson, *Washington Allston* (Chicago: University of Chicago Press, 1948), 112, 198; Gerdts and Stebbins, *Man of Genius*, 85; Crawford, 652.

[5] Grantz, no. 95, ii. 65–6. Grantz misread the first 'a' of the Barnard name as an 'e'.

Copies: 1. 46 × 36 in., presented to Jesus College in 1895 by its then Bursar, Hugh Shield (Crawford, 652).

2. Probably by Curnock, acquired by the Friends of Coleridge for Coleridge Cottage, 1996. (See *Coleridge Bulletin*, 7 (1996), 64.)

Later engravings: 1. Unsigned. Frontispiece of John Dix, *Pen and Ink Sketches of Poets, Preachers, and Politicians* (London: David Bogue, 1846). 3 ¼ × 4 inches. Caption: 'S. T. Coleridge [imitation signature]/ From a Sketch in Oils by Washington Allston'. Imprint: D Bogue. Fleet Street[.] The anonymous engraver has reduced Allston's three-quarter-length to half-length and given him a queasy expression.

2. By F. Croll, accompanying an article in *Hogg's Instructor* (copy in NYPL), NS 9 (1852), facing p. 129. This engraving is very similar to no. 1 above, but it cannot have been made from the same plate as the size of the face is larger and the style of the cravat distinctly different. Design area 4 (w.) × 3 15/16 in. (h.). Page 4 ½ × 7⅝ in. The engraving is signed 'F. Croll'; no artist's name appears. Caption: imitation signature 'S. T. Coleridge'. Imprint: 'Portrait Gallery of Hogg's Instructor[.]' The 'Portrait Gallery' was a regular feature of this publication; for this volume Croll also engraved portraits of James Montgomery and Barthold George Niebuhr, among others. The portraits accompanied essays on their subjects. The one on Coleridge (pp. 129–37, 152–7) is well informed and sympathetic.[6]

3. Mezzotint by Samuel Cousins (1801–87) published for George T. Barnard in 1854. 16½ × 12⅝ in. There are two states:[7] (1) Subscriber's proof (example in the BM Dept. of Prints and Drawings), with engraved inscription: 'Painted by Washington Allston. Engraved by Samuel Cousins, A.R.A. Subscriber's Proof.' (2) With the additional inscription: 'Samuel Taylor Coleridge. Aged 42. From the original Picture in the

[6] Haven, 142 (no. 1023), identifies the anonymous author as Peter Bayne, noting that Bayne reprinted this essay in his *Estimates of Some Englishmen and Some Scotchmen* (London, 1858).

[7] See Alfred Whitman, *Samuel Cousins* (London: George Bell & Sons, 1904), no. 41, pp. 55–6.

possession of George T. Barnard, Esq. London, Published July 10th 1854, by E. Moxon, 44 Dover Street.'

4. In the *Poems* of 1870, still edited by DC and SC and published by Moxon, the engraving after Shuter has been replaced by an unsigned engraving after the upper part of the 1814 Allston, showing the subject's head, shoulders, and cravat, which appears as the frontispiece. This fine stipple engraving measures $6\frac{9}{16} \times 4$ in.
5. Engraved frontispiece to Elbert Hubbard, *Little Journeys to the Homes of English Authors: S. T. Coleridge* (E. Aurora, NY: The Roycrofters, 1900), 7/11. No artist's name appears here, but the frontispiece to the Southey volume is inscribed 'P. Krame[?r]' and that of the Byron volume 'After the painting by Krämer.' It seems likely that P. Krämer executed copies after other artists, which were then engraved for the frontispieces of Hubbard's *Little Journeys*. Allston's three-quarter-length has been turned into a half-length.

16. **Charles Robert Leslie** (1794–1859)
1816.
Charcoal and white drawing on paper.
Dimensions unknown, but presumably similar to those of 16A.
Present location unknown.

Provenance: S. T. Coleridge, James Gillman, Anne Gillman, A. W. Gillman, Gillman family through A. H. Gillman.[8]

Literature: Charles Robert Leslie, *Autobiographical Recollections*, ed. Tom Taylor (2 vols.; London: John Murray, 1860), 199.

Reproduced: Gillman, *The Gillmans of Highgate*, facing p. 16. Signed on lower r.: 'Sketched by CRL / *1816*'; in lower centre 'M', probably for Meisenbach, the photographer responsible for a number of photographic reproductions of Coleridge portraits and other Coleridge-related material, including the Leslie portrait of James Gillman reproduced in this volume (facing

[8] An anonymous inscription on back of a photo of the drawing in the NPG reads: 'Coll: 1935 Mr. A. H. Gillman, a great-grandson of Coleridge's Highgate friend Gillman.'

p. 21). The Coleridge portrait is set in an oval—whether by the artist or for the reproduction is not known.

16A. Replica, possibly by C. R. Leslie
1816 or later.
Charcoal and white drawing on paper.
$7\frac{1}{8} \times 5\frac{7}{8}$ in.
Humanities Research Center, University of Texas.[9]
Provenance: S. T. Coleridge, Hartley Coleridge, Derwent Coleridge, E. H. Coleridge, Revd A. D. Coleridge, House of El Dieff, Inc.

17. **Charles Robert Leslie**
1818. (Later signed and dated 1820.)
Black pencil on blue-grey paper.
$10\frac{1}{2} \times 12\frac{1}{2}$ in.
Private collection.
Provenance: S. T. Coleridge, Derwent Coleridge, E. H. Coleridge, G. H. B. Coleridge, A. H. B. Coleridge.
Literature: *RP* i. 121; Crawford, 653–4.
Engravings: 1. By H. Meyer, *New Monthly Magazine*, 11 (1 Apr. 1819), facing p. 240 (in reverse, subject looking to the viewer's right). Signatures: 'Drawn by C. R. Leslie Engraved by H. Meyer.' Caption: 'S. T. Coleridge, Esq.'; Imprint: 'Published April 1, 1819 by Henry Colburn, Conduit Street[.]' Page size: $4\frac{7}{8} \times 7\frac{1}{2}$ in. Image within ruled bounds: $4\frac{1}{4} \times 5\frac{1}{2}$ in. The BM Dept. of Prints and Drawings has an example on a separate sheet (not necessarily a separate plate). This beautifully executed engraving may have been the prototype for several subsequent ones.

[9] A note in the hand of EHC filed with the picture at the HRC reads: 'This crayon drawing of S. T. Coleridge—formerly in the possession of Derwent Coleridge—and kept *I think*, in Hartley Coleridge's desk is evidently a copy or, more frankly, a replica of a sketch by C. R. Leslie, R. A., taken in 1816 (see his Letter June 3, 1816 *Autobiographical Recollections*, 1860, ii. 50) which is reproduced in the *Gillmans of Highgate*, to face p. 16. It differs from a sketch taken by Leslie circ. 1820, which is in my possession—This larger sketch was published by H. Colburn in the European Magazine—Ap 2. 1819 [words illegible] in *1828*, so it must have been copied by Leslie or else [words illegible] May 21, 1914.' Also with the picture is a trade card from frame maker W. W. Izzard, Aylesbury. This portrait, unlike the reproduction of 19, is not set in an oval.

2. By R. Cooper in the *Literary Speculum*, 2 (1822), facing p. 145. This appears to be a very free adaptation after Meyer. (It could, of course, have been engraved directly after the Leslie drawing itself, but special arrangements would have been necessary for that.) Like the Meyer engraving, it is reversed (head turned to our left). The signature is 'R. Cooper, Sc.' (no artist's name given) and the caption 'S. T. Coleridge, Esq.' Imprint: 'London: Published by T. Richardson, 98 High Holborn.' The image is boxed by two ruled lines, one double and one single, set in an ornate engraved frame. Size (measuring from the inner ruled line): $2\frac{11}{16}$ in. (h.) × $2\frac{1}{4}$ in. (w.). This engraving accompanies a generally sympathetic article 'On the Poetry of Coleridge', pp. 145–51, signed 'R'. Examples on loose sheets (but not necessarily separate plates) are in the NPG archive and in an extra-illustrated copy of a biography of Edward Bulwer-Lytton in the HEH (no. 131334, vol. 2).). Measurements of the latter are: Image inside rule: $2\frac{7}{8}$ × $2\frac{3}{8}$ in. Image including engraved 'frame': $4\frac{1}{14}$ × $3\frac{3}{8}$ in. Platemark: $7\frac{13}{16}$ × $4\frac{3}{4}$ in. Leaf: $8\frac{7}{8}$ × $5\frac{1}{2}$ in.
3. By an unknown engraver, published by William Darton in 1823. This is very like the Cooper engraving, and may also be based on Henry Meyer's engraving, but a curtain and a bookcase with books have been added behind the subject. On card, $4\frac{3}{5}$ × $3\frac{3}{25}$ in. With a short text, including 'His poetical works have experienced a very flattering reception and his monody on the death of Chatterton has been much admired.' According to Crawford, 654, this is 'one of a collection of similar cards of famous people'.
4. By James Hopwood, in Amédée Pichot, *Voyage historique en Angleterre* (Paris: Saunders & Ottley 1825), ii. 394/5. A fine engraving, capturing the gleam in Coleridge's eye, this may be after Meyer but shows a good deal more of Coleridge's jacket and vest. Signatures: 'Leslie pinx. Hopwood sculp.' Four ruled borders frame the image. Caption: facsimile signature, 'S. T. Coleridge.' Imprint: 'imprimé par Lemarchand fils[.]' Measurements: to first ruled border, $4\frac{1}{16}$ × 3 in. Leaf: 8 × 5 in.

5. By an unknown engraver, a proof before shading, inscribed 'Mr. Coleridge[.]' Undated. Sheet $6\frac{1}{16} \times 3\frac{7}{8}$ in. In NYPL, Dept. of Prints and Drawings.

18. **Thomas Phillips** (1770–1845)
1818–21.
Oil.
$35 \times 27\frac{1}{2}$ in.
Private collection.
Provenance: Bishop William Hart Coleridge, Coleridge family.

18A. Replica by Thomas Phillips
Completed 1835.
Oil.
36×28 in.
John Murray collection.
Provenance: John Murray.
Exhibitions: Manchester Art Treasures Exhib., 1857; National Portrait Exhib., South Kensington, 1868; New Gallery (Guelph), 1891.
Engravings (posthumous): 1. Lithograph by Louis Haghe (1806–85). 1835. $6\frac{5}{8} \times 5\frac{3}{8}$ in. Captioned with a facsimile imitation signature: 'dear Sir/Your obliged Servnt/S. T. Coleridge.' 2. Zinc engraving by Louis Haghe. 1835. $5\frac{1}{4} \times 3\frac{9}{16}$ in. Same caption. 3. Lithograph by E. F. Finden. Dated 1837 in the imprint although the second edition of *Table Talk*, of which it is the frontispiece, bears the date 1836 on its title page. Same caption. $6\frac{3}{8} \times 3\frac{3}{4}$ in. These prints were executed in connection with the first and second editions of *Table Talk* (1835, 1836).
Literature: *RP* i. 121; Crawford, 654.

19. **Charles Mottram** (1806–76)
*c.*1823–4.
Engraving after drawings by John Doyle (1797–1868), mixed method.
$26\frac{1}{2} \times 35\frac{3}{4}$ in.

An example in the V & A, Pressmark 19. c. 2. CT 17330, Accession no. E 734–1940. Inscribed in pencil at lower right: 'Artist's Proof' and signed 'Charles Mottram'; facsimile signatures of all persons shown. Another example in the Tate Gallery.

Engraved legends: at lower left, 'Pedestal carved by Sir Francis L. Chantrey, R. A.'; at centre, 'Anno 1815.'

Literature: David Blayney Brown, 'New Light on "H. B.": An Early Work by John Doyle', *Print Quarterly*, 2 (1985), 48–9; Tate Gallery, *Illustrated Catalogue of Acquisitions* (1986–8), 18 (no. T 04907).

20. **Edward Villiers Rippingille** (1798–1859)
1824.
Oil on panel.
$32\frac{3}{8} \times 52\frac{5}{8}$ in.
Clevedon Court, Somerset (National Trust).

Provenance: Sir Charles Abraham Elton; Sir Arthur Elton; John Gibbons; Mrs John Gibbons; Christie's 17 Mar. 1883 (no. 119).

Exhibition: Bristol, 1824; RA 1824.

Literature: *RP* i. 121; Arthur and Margaret Ann Elton, *Guide to Clevedon Court* (London: The National Trust, 1972), 133–6; Francis Greenacre, *The Bristol School of Artists* (Bristol: Bristol Art Gallery, 1973), 133–5; Crawford, 654.

Other versions: An oil study was exhibited at the Bristol Institution in 1826. It was purchased by Charles Hare and according to Greenacre may have been owned by E. V. Rippingille, Jun. The artist attempted to sell by lottery a second version (present location unknown), executed with the assistance of his brother Alex, between 1826 and 1830. According to Francis Greenacre, this version showed 'some alterations in the figures'.[10]

Engravings: By F. C. Lewis, 1837. Unsigned engraving dated 1877 (Coleridge Cottage). Title: 'The Early Breakfast'. Printed by

[10] 'Missing Copy of a Painting', *Country Life*, 156 (no. 4039, 1974), 1660.

T. Brooker. Facial expressions have been completely changed to caricature, and comic details, such as someone stealing the egg, have been added.

21. **J. G. Spurzheim** (1776–1832)
1825.
Plaster.
Measurements:[11] Greatest circumference: 24 $\frac{6}{25}$ ins. From occipital spine to tip of nasal bone, over the vertex: 15 in. From ear to ear, over the vertex: 15 in. Point of chin to vertex (in vertical plane): 10 in. Maximum width of head (made with calipers): 6 $\frac{1}{2}$ in.
Henderson Trust, Department of Anatomy, University of Edinburgh.
Provenance: Edinburgh Phrenological Society.
Exhibition: *Death Masks and Life Masks of the Famous and Infamous*, Scotland's Cultural Heritage.
Literature: Catalogue for the above, Foreword by M. H. Kaufman, Professor of Anatomy, University of Edinburgh; Carl Woodring, *TT* i. 184 n. 14; Eric C. Walker, 'Reading Proof, *Aids to Reflection*, and Phrenology: A New Coleridge Letter', *European Romantic Review*, 8/3 (1997), 323–40.

21A. ?Warren Anatomical Museum, Harvard University.
Provenance: Boston Phrenological Society.
Literature: *A Catalogue of Phrenological Specimens Belonging to the Boston Phrenological Society* (Boston: Printed by John Ford, 1835); J. B. S. Jackson MD, *Harvard University: A Descriptive of the Warren Anatomical Museum* (Boston: A. Williams and Co., 1870).

22. **Catherina de Predl** (1790–1871)
*c.*1826.
Chalk or pastel drawing.

[11] Kindly taken by Prof. M. H. Kaufman, University of Edinburgh Medical School. Professor Kaufman notes that mask measurements invariably tend to be greater than those taken during life.

Present location unknown.
Measurements unknown.
Literature: *Hampstead and Highgate Express*, Oct. 1972; Eric W. Nye, 'A Portrait of the Sage At Highgate', *Wordsworth Circle*, 13 (1982), 231–2; *RP* i. 121; Crawford, 655.
Copies 1. Oil copy. 29 × 24 in. Private collection. *Provenance*: Mrs E. G. Robinson. 2. Oil copy. 28 × 23 in. Highgate Literary and Scientific Institution. *Provenance*: James Gillman, Robert G. Moger, Maria Moger, Sir Ambrose Heal, Lady Heal.
Exhibition: *Coleridge and Highgate*, Highgate Scientific and Literary Institution, 1983.

23. **Moses Haughton** (1774–1848)
1832.
Oil.
$29\frac{4}{5} \times 24\frac{4}{5}$ in.
Christ's Hospital, Horsham.
Provenance: Jonathan Green, Mary Green (his daughter).
Literature: *RP* i. 121; Crawford, 656–7.
Exhibition: Royal Albert Memorial Museum, Exeter, 1934 (no. 3, 'Artist Unknown'). A gilded plaque at the base of the picture reads: 'The gift of Jonathan Green MD deceased 1864.'

23A. Copy of the portrait by Moses Haughton by an unknown artist
1832 or later.
Oil on canvas.
$35\frac{3}{8} \times 27\frac{3}{4}$ in.
Humanities Research Center, University of Texas.
Provenance: Joseph Henry Green, Mrs J. H. Green, Derwent Coleridge, E. H. Coleridge, G. H. B. Coleridge, A. H. B. Coleridge.
Exhibition: Royal Albert Memorial Museum, Exeter, 1934 (no. 2, 'Painted by an unknown artist at the Argyll Baths'). No resemblance between this picture and the Haughton portrait (also in this exhibition) is remarked in the catalogue.

Literature: Anon., 'Coleridge Centenary Exhibition', *New Statesman and Nation*, NS 8 (1934), 153; Crawford, 656.

24. **Daniel Maclise** (1806–70)
1833.
Pencil drawing.
Victoria and Albert Museum.
$9\frac{3}{8} \times 4\frac{1}{4}$ in.
Provenance: John Forster.
Signed with monogram M over D in lower l. and in lower r. inscribed: 'S. T. Coleridge / from Life / Highgate / D. M.'. About midway to the right is a word that could be 'attitude' followed by 'o' (the rest could have been cut off).
Copy: undated, by an unknown artist, in Wordsworth Museum, Grasmere. $7\frac{3}{4} \times 5\frac{1}{2}$ in. Initials WRG on mount.
Engraving: Lithograph by Daniel Maclise[12] for *Fraser's Magazine*, 8 (July 1833), facing p. 64 (repr. *RP* ii. pl. 1602). Right signature: 'A. Croquis del.' (Croquis was Maclise's pseudonym.) 'Samuel Taylor Coleridge, Esq.' Engr. page size $8\frac{7}{8} \times 7\frac{3}{8}$ in. Caption: 'S. T. Coleridge' (facsimile of signature) and underneath it 'AUTHOR OF "CHRISTABEL" '.
Posthumous: William Bates, *The Maclise Portrait Gallery* (London: Chatto & Windus, 1873). Coleridge also appears posthumously in an engraving after Maclise's drawing *The Fraserians* (Forster Collection, V. & A.), *Fraser's* 11 (Jan. 1835), double spread preceding p. 1 (repr. *RP* ii. pl. 1602). The V. & A. has two pencil drawings for this: the larger one is $8\frac{1}{4} \times 10\frac{3}{4}$ in., the smaller $7\frac{7}{8} \times 5\frac{1}{4}$ in.
Exhibition: National Portrait Gallery, London, and National Gallery of Ireland, Dublin, 1972.
Literature: Richard Ormond, *Daniel Maclise* (exhibition catalogue, London: Arts Council, 1972), 48, no. 49.

[12] *British Portraits Preserved in the Department of Prints and Drawings*, i. 464–5.

25. **J. Kayser** (1813–53)
Signed 'J. Kayser/ 1833'.
Pencil drawing.
$7\frac{7}{8} \times 6\frac{1}{2}$ in.
Private collection.
Provenance: Samuel Taylor Coleridge, (?Joseph Henry Green), Mrs Joseph Henry Green, DC, EHC, A. H. B. Coleridge. Presumably it was either paid for by Joseph Henry Green or given to him as a present by Coleridge.
Literature: Crawford, 657; M. D. Paley, *Coleridge's Later Poetry* (Oxford: Clarendon, 1996), 132.

26. **Abraham Wivell** (1786–1849)
1833.
Presumably a pencil or crayon drawing.
Measurements unknown.
Location unknown.
Engraving: By W. Wagstaff for *Finden's Illustrations of the Life and Works of Lord Byron* (London: John Murray), iii. n. p., preceding short article entitled 'S. T. Coleridge' by W. Brockedon. Page size $8\frac{3}{4} \times 7\frac{1}{2}$ in. On the NYPL impression, someone has inscribed 'India paper proof scarce[.]' Later re-engraved by T. G. Welch for *The Works of Samuel Taylor Coleridge* (Philadelphia, 1840) and by J. F. E. Prudhomme for *The Complete Works*, ed. Shedd (1853, frontispiece to vol. i). Also frontispiece to the 1871 and 1884 edns (7 vols.; New York: Harper & Bros.).
Literature: *RP* i. 122; Crawford, 657; Paley, *Coleridge's's Later Poetry*, 132–3.

5
Supplementary Notes

A. Coleridge Masks in the Warren Anatomical Museum[1]

Three masks of Coleridge, two life-masks and a death-mask, are listed by J. B. S. Jackson MD in *Harvard University: A Descriptive Catalogue of the Warren Anatomical Museum*,[2] under the category 'Miscellany' and the Subcategory 'Series XLIV.—Phrenology'. Unfortunately, the Warren Museum collections are not accessible at the time of writing, having been removed and stored off-site for eventual reinstallation in the Countway Library of Medicine (Boston). It has therefore not been possible to examine the masks or to obtain photographs of them.

A headnote in the *Descriptive Catalogue*, p. 710, says that most of the specimens in this section were collected by the Boston Phrenological Society. After its existence ended, Dr J. C. Warren purchased them and presented them to the Medical College in 1847. 'The first specimens were from the Collections of Dr Spurzheim, and of Mr J. D. Holm, London . . .' The entries are as follows, with an asterisk indicating a life-mask:

3337. *Samuel Taylor Coleridge, cast in 1810.
3338. * " " 1821.
3339. * " " July, 1834.
Biography in Galignani's edition of poetical works.

The Boston Phrenological Society, from which these masks were obtained, was founded by a group of admirers and disciples of J. G. Spurzheim immediately after Spurzheim's death in Boston in 1832.[3] In

[1] My attention was drawn to the existence of these masks by Prof. Matthew Kaufman, Curator of the Henderson Trust Collection, University of Edinburgh. Further information and photocopies were kindly furnished by Madeleine W. Mullin (Reference Librarian at the Francis A. Countway Library of Medicine, Boston) and by Dr Aaron Paul (Curator of the Warren Museum Collections).

[2] (Boston: A. Williams & Co., 1870), 710.

[3] See J. Collins Warren MD, 'The Collection of the Boston Phrenological Society—A Retrospect', *Annals of Medical History*, 3 (1921), 1–11. According to this article, Dr J. C.

the catalogue of its collection published by the Society in 1835,[4] the Coleridge entries are to be found under 'Triplicates' (p. 4) in the section headed: 'Specimens from the Collections of the Late Dr. Spurzheim and J. D. Holm' (p. 2). The three masks are listed as follows, with an asterisk indicating a mask rather than a whole head:

*20	Samuel Taylor Coleridge, cast in 1810.		
21	do	do	1827, aet. 54.
22	do	after death, July, 1834.	

It is very possible that the first item (Warren 3337) is the life-mask taken by George Dawe in 1811 (Cat. 12), or a cast taken from it, with the date advanced by one year. This likelihood is strengthened by the listing immediately after the third Coleridge entry in both catalogues of '*William Godwin, cast in 1805, by G. Dawe.'[5] The second mask (Warren 3338) may possibly be a previously unknown cast of Coleridge's head (as the failure to star it in the Boston *Catalogue*, no. 21, would suggest). However, if this specimen came from Spurzheim's own collection, it is very possible that it is the life-mask taken by Spurzheim himself, or a cast from it, now dated 1825 by recently discovered circumstantial evidence (see pp. 82–3 and Cat. 21). In that case no. 3338 may require redating. The catalogue entry reads '1827, aet. fifty-four', but as Coleridge was born in 1771 and therefore was 54 in 1825, there is at least some possibility that the Warren Collection mask and the Henderson Trust mask are casts from the same matrix (or, alternatively that one is

Warren had known Spurzheim during the period that Spurzheim spent in Boston (where he died of typhoid in 1832). 'Dr. Warren used many of the preparations of the Phrenological Society in his lectures and . . . a large number of skulls and casts were loaned to him by the society for this purpose.' (Whether any of the Coleridge masks was so used is not mentioned.) The article also reprints documents by which the collection that had belonged to the Boston Phrenological Society was transferred to Dr J. C. Warren.

[4] *A Catalogue of Phrenological Specimens Belonging to the Boston Phrenological Society* (Boston: Printed by John Ford, 1835).

[5] Boston Phrenological Society *Catalogue*, p. 4, no. *23; Warren Museum *Descriptive Catalogue*, p. 711, no. *3340. This is followed by a head of Godwin cast in August 1830 and supposedly showing 'Increase in the organ of Benevolence' (Boston *Catalogue*, p. 4, no. 24; Warren Museum *Descriptive Catalogue*, no. *3340. Among other notable Boston specimens (pp. 2–5) are: three heads of Spurzheim from different dates, one of Gall, 'Jeremy Bentham after Death, July 19, 1832', two of F. Mendelssohn Bartholdy (in entry no. 35, cast in 1829, 'Grandson of the Philosopher Moses Mendelssohn', in no. 36, 'July 1833', aet. 24: 'Amateur Musical composer'); there are also masks of Napoleon, Cromwell, Lord Chatham, William Pitt, and Horne Tooke. All these passed into the collection of the Warren Anatomical Museum.

a matrix and the other a cast from it). The third, though also unstarred in the Boston *Catalogue*, is very likely to be a cast of the death-mask made for Dr Gillman (see pp. 109–11) above).

B. Missing, Unidentified, or Non-Existent Portraits

1. A portrait by Alexander Geddes (1783–1844) was projected in 1826. Coleridge wrote to his nephew Edward on 8 February 1826: 'The weather must improve & the days lengthen before I can with any chance of repeating my visit wait on Mr. Geddes; but you may depend on my calling the first time I go to town, and endeavoring to arrange my sittings.'[6] No portrait by Geddes is known to have been produced.

2. In the British Museum Department of Prints and Drawings album of Burney Theatrical Portraits, xii. 109, no. 193, there is a small unsigned engraving with the caption 'Coleridge'. It might possibly be a book frontispiece, but it has not been possible to identify it further.

3. Arthur Hugh Clough reported when an undergraduate at Oxford, in 1841: 'By the bye, there is a new and as seems to me very striking portrait of him [Coleridge] just published by Holloway, Henrietta Street, Covent Garden, which I have seen in our Coleridge's rooms and which he says is by those who knew him to be the best by far there exists and I can easily believe it.'[7] Clough was at Balliol College and so was John Duke Coleridge, but this engraving has yet to be identified. A print publisher named M. M. Holloway flourished in the 1840s to 1850s,[8] but no portrait engraving of Coleridge published by him has been found.

[6] *CL* vi. 561. Some portrait engravings after paintings by Geddes are discussed by Kenneth Sanderson in 'Engravings After Andrew Geddes', *Print Collectors Quarterly*, 16 (1929), 109–31.

[7] Letter to J. N. Simkinson dated 16 Feb. 1841, *The Correspondence of Arthur Hugh Clough* (Oxford: Clarendon, 1957), i. 106.

[8] See Raymond Lister, *Prints and Printmaking: A Dictionary and Handbook of the Art in Nineteenth-Century Britain* (London: Methuen, 1984), 230.

Bibliography

A Catalogue of Phrenological Specimens Belonging to the Boston Phrenological Society (Boston: Printed by John Ford, 1835).

ALBRIGHT, RAYMOND, *Focus on Infinity: A Life of Phillips Brooks* (New York: Macmillan, 1961).

ALCOTT, AMOS BRONSON, *The Journals of Bronson Alcott*, ed. Odell Shephard (Boston: Little, Brown, 1938).

ALLEN, GAY WILSON, 'The Iconography of Walt Whitman', in *The Artistic Legacy of Walt Whitman*, ed. Edwin Haviland Miller (New York: New York University Press, 1970), 127–57.

ALLSTON, WASHINGTON, *The Correspondence of Washington Allston*, ed. Nathalia Wright (Lexington, Ky.: University Press of Kentucky, 1993).

ANON., 'Coleridge by Opie?' *Country Life*, 154 (1973), 1537.

—— 'How Great Men Really Looked', *Life*, 22 Dec. 1952, p. 74.

—— 'Coleridge Centenary Exhibition', *The New Statesman and Nation*, NS 8 (1934), 153.

—— Exhibition Catalogue *S. T. Coleridge: Centenary Exhibition Organized by the University College of the South West of England*, Royal Albert Memorial Museum, Exeter, July–Oct. 1934. Preface by Humphry House, pp. 4–6.

[BARNARD, GEORGE TOVEY], untitled prospectus promoting the engraving by Samuel Cousins after Washington Allston (London, 1853).

BATE, WALTER JACKSON, *John Keats* (Cambridge, Mass.: Harvard University Press, 1963).

BEERBOHM, MAX, *The Poets' Corner* (London: Heinemann, 1904).

BENKARD, ERNEST, *Undying Faces: A Collection of Death Masks*, trans. Margaret M. Green (London: Hogarth, 1929).

BENTLEY, G. E., Jr., *Blake Records* (Oxford: Clarendon, 1969).

BETHAM, ERNEST, *A House of Letters*, 2nd edn. (London: Jarrold & Sons, ?1905).

BINDMAN, DAVID (ed.), *The Thames and Hudson Encyclopaedia of British Art* (London: Thames & Hudson, 1985).

BLAKE, WILLIAM, *Complete Poetry and Prose*, ed. David V. Erdman, rev. edn. (Berkeley and Los Angeles: University of California Press, 1982).

BLANSHARD, FRANCES, *Portraits of Wordsworth* (London: George Allen & Unwin, 1959).

BLUNDEN, EDMUND, Letter to the *Times Literary Supplement*, 14 February 1935, p. 92.

Bookman, The (London), 26 (1904, special Coleridge issue), 185–209.

BRILLIANT, RICHARD, *Portraiture* (London: Reaktion Books, 1991).

BROCKEDON, WILLIAM, *Finden's Illustrations of the Life and Works of Lord Byron* (3 vols.; London: J. Murray, 1833–4).

BRYAN, MICHAEL, *Biographical and Critical Dictionary of Painters and Engravers*, rev. and enlarged by George Stanley (London: H. S. Bohn, 1853).

—— *Bryan's Dictionary of Painters and Engravers*, rev. and enlarged by George C. Williamson (London: George Bell & Sons, 1905).

BURKE, JOSEPH, *English Art 1714–1800* (Oxford: Clarendon, 1976).

BURTON, ANTHONY, and MURDOCH, JOHN, *Byron: An Exhibition to Commemorate the Anniversary of his Death in the Greek War of Liberation, 19 April 1824* (London: V. & A., 1974).

BYRON, LORD, *The Complete Poetical Works*, ed. Jerome J. McGann (6 vols.; Oxford: Clarendon, 1980–93).

CAM, WALTER H., 'A Coleridge Portrait', *TLS* (1935), 92.

CAMERON, KENNETH WALTER, 'Emerson's "Capital Print" of Coleridge,' *Emerson Society Quarterly*, 2 (1956), 8–9.

CARLYLE, THOMAS, *The Life of John Sterling* (New York: Charles Scribner's Sons, 1900).

CARPENTER, EDWARD, *A House of Kings: The Official History of Westminster Abbey* (New York: John Day, 1966).

CHORLEY, HENRY F., *The Authors of England* (London: Charles Tilt, 1838).

CLARKE, CHARLES and MARY COWDEN, *Recollections of Writers* (New York: Charles Scribner's Sons, 1878).

CLIFFORD, T., 'The Plaster Shops of the Rococo and Neoclassical Era in Britain', *Journal of the History of Collections*, 4 (1992), 39–65.

CLOUGH, ARTHUR HUGH, *The Correspondence of Arthur Hugh Clough*, ed. Frederick L. Mulhauser (2 vols.; Oxford: Clarendon, 1957).

COBURN, K., *In Pursuit of Coleridge* (London: Bodley Head, 1977).

—— 'Notes on Washington Allston from the Unpublished Notebooks of S. T. Coleridge', *Gazette des Beaux-Arts*, 25 (1944), 249–52.

COLERIDGE, BERNARD JOHN SEYMOUR, *The Story of a Devonshire House* (London: T. Fisher Unwin, 1905).

COLERIDGE, ERNEST HARTLEY, MS notes on Coleridge portraits, MS 79.360, Harry Ransom Center for the Humanities, University of Texas, Austin.

COLERIDGE, HENRY NELSON, MS correspondence, BL Add. MSS 35344–47557; John Murray Archive (London).

COLERIDGE, Sir JOHN DUKE, *Life and Correspondence of John Duke Lord Coleridge*, ed. E. H. Coleridge (2 vols.; London: Heinemann, 1904).

COLERIDGE, SAMUEL TAYLOR, *Biographia Literaria*, CC 7, ed. James Engell and W. Jackson Bate (2 vols.; Princeton: Princeton University Press, 1983).

—— *Collected Letters of Samuel Taylor Coleridge*, ed. Earl Leslie Griggs (6 vols.; Oxford and New York: Oxford University Press, 1956–71).

—— *Complete Poetical Works*, ed. E. H. Coleridge (2 vols.; Oxford: Clarendon, 1912).

—— *Lectures 1808–1819 on Literature*, CC 5, ed. R. A. Foakes (2 vols.; Princeton: Princeton University Press, 1987).

—— *Letters*, ed. E. H. Coleridge (2 vols.; London: Heinemann, 1895).

—— *The Notebooks of Samuel Taylor Coleridge*, ed. Kathleen Coburn (Princeton: Princeton University Press, 1957–).

—— *Poems*, ed. John Beer (London: J. M. Dent, rev. edn. 1993).

—— *Shorter Works and Fragments*, ed. H. J. and J. R. de J. Jackson, CC 11 (Princeton: Princeton University Press, 1995).

—— *Table Talk*, CC 14, ed. Carl Woodring (2 vols.; Princeton: Princeton University Press, 1990).

COLERIDGE, SARA, *Sara Coleridge and Henry Reed*, ed. Leslie Nathan Broughton (Ithaca, NY: Cornell University Press, 1937).

COOK, CYRIL, 'A Pioneer in Porcelain Decoration,' *Country Life*, 26 (January 1951), 250–1.

COTTLE, JOSEPH, *Early Recollections* (2 vols., London, 1837).

CRAWFORD, WALTER B., with the assistance of CRAWFORD, ANNE, *Samuel Taylor Coleridge: An Annotated Bibliography of Criticism and Scholarship*, iii (Boston: G. K. Hall., 1996).

CRAWFORD, WALTER B., and LAUTERBACH, EDWARD S., *Samuel Taylor Coleridge: An Annotated Bibliography of Criticism and Scholarship*, ii (Boston: G. K. Hall, 1983).

DE QUINCEY, THOMAS, *The Collected Writings of Thomas De Quincey* (14 vols.; Edinburgh: Adam & Charles Black, 1880).

De Quincey, Thomas, *Recollections of the Lake Poets*, ed. David Wright (Harmondsworth: Penguin, 1970).

—— *Selections Grave and Gay, from Writings Published and Unpublished* (14 vols.; Edinburgh: James Hogg, 1853–60).

Dibdin, Thomas, *Reminiscences of a Literary Life* (2 vols.; London: John Major, 1836).

Dix, John, *Pen and Ink Sketches of Poets, Preachers, and Politicians* (London: David Bogue, 1846).

Drazan, Joseph Gerald and Sanguine, Phyllis, *An Index to the Caricatures in* The New York Review of Books *from Its Inception Through the Fifteenth Anniversary Issue (1963–1978)* (Walla Walla, Wash.: Penrose Memorial Library, Whitman College, 1978).

Dunlap, William, *History of the Arts of Design in the United States* (2 vols.; New York: Scott, 1834).

Elton, Arthur and Margaret Ann, *Guide to Clevedon Court* (London: National Trust, 1972).

Emerson, Ralph Waldo, *The Letters of Ralph Waldo Emerson*, ed. Ralph L. Rusk (6 vols.; New York: Columbia University Press, 1939), i. 397.

Engell, James (ed.), *Coleridge: The Early Family Letters* (Oxford: Clarendon, 1994).

Erdman, David V., 'Unrecorded Coleridge Variants', *Studies in Bibliography*, 11 (1958), 143–62.

Farington, Joseph, *The Diary of Joseph Farington*, ed. Kenneth Garlick and Angus Macintyre (16 vols.; New Haven and London: Yale University Press, 1978–84).

Flagg, Jared B., *The Life and Letters of Washington Allston* (New York: Charles Scribner's Sons, 1892).

Gerdts, William H., and Stebbins, Theodore E., Jr., *'A Man of Genius': The Art of Washington Allston* (Boston: Museum of Fine Arts, 1979).

Gill, Stephen, *William Wordsworth: A Life* (Oxford: Clarendon, 1989).

Gillman, A. W., *The Gillmans of Highgate and S. T. Coleridge* (London: Elliot Stock, 1895).

—— *The Life of Samuel Taylor Coleridge* (London: W. Pickering, 1834).

Gittings, Robert, *Claire Clairmont and the Shelleys* (Oxford and New York: Oxford University Press, 1992).

—— *The Mask of Keats* (Cambridge, Mass.: Harvard University Press, 1956).

GOODISON, J. W., 'Cambridge Portraits, IV: Later Nineteenth and Twentieth Centuries', *Connoisseur*, 144 (1959), 8–13.

GRANTZ, CARL L., 'Letters of Sara Coleridge: A Calendar and Index to Her Manuscript Correspondence in the University of Texas Library', 2 vols., Ph.D. diss., University of Texas at Austin, 1968 (Ann Arbor, Mich.: University Microfilms, 1968).

GRATTAN, THOMAS COLLEY, *Beaten Paths and Those Who Trod Them* (2 vols.; London: Chapman & Hall, 1862).

GRAVES, ALGERNON, *A Century of Loan Exhibitions 1813–1912* (5 vols.; London: Algernon Graves, 1913).

—— *Dictionary of Artists Who Have Exhibited Works in the Principal London Exhibitions from 1760 to 1893* (New York: Burt Franklin, 1970 (1901)).

—— *The Royal Academy of Arts: A Complete Dictionary of Contributors and their Work from its Foundation in 1769 to 1904* (8 vols.; New York: Burt Franklin, 1972 (1905–6)).

GREENACRE, FRANCIS, *The Bristol School of Artists: Francis Danby and Painting in Bristol* (Bristol: City Art Gallery, 1973).

—— 'Missing Copy of a Painting', *Country Life*, 156, no. 4039 (1974), 1660.

GRIGGS, E. L., *Coleridge Fille: A Biography of Sara Coleridge* (London: Oxford University Press, 1940).

GUNNIS, RUPERT, *Dictionary of British Sculptors 1660–1851* (London: Odhams, 1968).

HALL, S. C., *A Book of Memories of Great Men and Women of the Age, from Personal Acquaintance* (London: Virtue, 1871).

HANEY, JOHN LOUIS, *A Bibliography of Samuel Taylor Coleridge* (Philadelphia: privately printed, 1903).

HAVEN, RICHARD, HAVEN, JOSEPHINE, and ADAMS, MAURIANNE, *Samuel Taylor Coleridge: An Annotated Bibliography of Criticism and Scholarship*, i (Boston: G. K. Hall, 1976).

HAYES, JOHN, *The Portrait in British Art* (London: National Portrait Gallery, 1991).

HAYLEY, WILLIAM, *The Life of George Romney, Esq.* (Chichester, 1809).

HAYTER, ALETHEA, *A Voyage in Vain: Coleridge's Journey to Malta in 1804* (London: Faber & Faber, 1973).

HAZLITT, W. CAREW, *Four Generations of a Literary Family* (4 vols.; London: George Redway, 1897).

—— *Memoirs of William Hazlitt* (2 vols.; London, 1867).

HAZLITT, WILLIAM, *The Complete Works of William Hazlitt*, ed. P. P. Howe (21 vols.; London and Toronto: J. M. Dent, 1930–4).

HOLMES, RICHARD, *Coleridge: Early Visions* (London: Hodder & Stoughton, 1989).

—— 'The Romantic Circle', *New York Review of Books*, 44 (10 Apr. 1997), 34–5.

—— *Shelley: The Pursuit* (London: Quartet, 1976).

HORACE, *The Odes and Epodes*, trans. C. E. Bennett (Cambridge, Mass.: Harvard University Press, 1988).

HOUGHTON, WALTER E., *The Wellesley Index to Victorian Periodicals 1824–1900* (5 vols.; Toronto: University of Toronto Press, 1966–89).

HOWE, P. P., *Life of William Hazlitt* (Harmondsworth: Penguin, 1949).

HUNT, LEIGH, *The Autobiography of Leigh Hunt* (3 vols.; London: Smith, Elder & Co., 1850).

—— *Lord Byron and Some of His Contemporaries* (London: Henry Colburn, 1828).

HUTTON, LAURENCE, 'A Collection of Death Masks', *Harper's New Monthly Magazine*, 85 (1892).

—— *Talks in a Library*, recorded by Isabel Moore (New York: G. P. Putnam's Sons, 1905).

HYMAN, SUZANNE K., 'Contemporary Portraits of Byron', in *Lord Byron and His Contemporaries*, ed. Charles E. Robinson (Newark, Del.: University of Delaware Press, 1982), 207–8.

JACKSON, J. B. S., MD, *Harvard University: A Descriptive Catalogue of the Warren Anatomical Museum* (Boston: A. Williams and Co., 1870).

KEATS, JOHN, *The Letters of John Keats, 1814–1821*, ed. Hyder Edward Rollins (2 vols.; Cambridge, Mass.: Harvard University Press, 1958).

—— *The Poems of John Keats*, ed. Jack Stillinger (Cambridge, Mass.: Harvard University Press, 1978).

KEYNES, Sir GEOFFREY, *The Complete Portraiture of William and Catherine Blake* (London: Trianon/William Blake Trust, 1977).

KILMURRAY, ELAINE, *Dictionary of British Portraiture* (London: B. T. Batsford, 1979).

KRAMM, CHRISTIAN, *De Levens en Werken der Hallandische en Vlamsche Kunstschilders, Beeldhouwers, Graveurs, en Bouwmeesters . . .* (Amsterdam, 1859), pt. 3, p. 841.

LAMB, CHARLES, *The Letters of Charles Lamb, to Which Are Added Those of His Sister, Mary Lamb*, ed. E. V. Lucas (3 vols.; London: Methuen, 1935).

LAMB, CHARLES and MARY, *Letters*, ed. E. W. Marrs, Jr. (3 vols.; Ithaca, NY: Cornell University Press, 1975).

—— *The Works of Charles and Mary Lamb*, ed. E. V. Lucas (7 vols.; London: J. M. Dent & Methuen, 1935).

LEFEBURE, MOLLY, *The Bondage of Love* (London: Victor Gollancz, 1987).

—— *Samuel Taylor Coleridge: A Bondage of Opium* (New York: Stein & Day, 1974).

Leicester Museum and Art Gallery, '. . . *a painter's eye, a poet's heart': Sir George Beaumont of Coleorton, Leicestershire* (Leicester, 1974).

LESLIE, CHARLES ROBERT, *Autobiographical Reflections*, ed. Tom Taylor (2 vols.; London: John Murray, 1860).

LINDOP, GREVEL, *The Opium-Eater: A Life of Thomas De Quincey* (Oxford: Oxford University Press, 1985).

LISTER, RAYMOND, *Prints and Printmaking: A Dictionary and Handbook of the Art in Nineteenth-Century Britain* (London: Methuen, 1984).

LOWELL, ROBERT, *Life Studies*, 2nd edn. (London: Faber & Faber, 1968).

MACLEAN, CATHERINE MACDONALD, *Born Under Saturn: A Biography of William Hazlitt* (London: Collins, 1943).

MARTINEAU, HARRIET, *Harriet Martineau's Autobiography*, ed. Marcia Weston Chapman (Boston: James R. Osgood, 1877).

—— *Harriet Martineau's Autobiography*, with a new Introduction by Gaby Weiner (2 vols.; London: Virago, 1983).

MOGER, MARIA W., MS Letters to and from, Highgate Literary and Scientific Institution Archive.

MOORE, DORIS LANGLEY, 'Byronic Dress', *Costume*, 5 (1971), 1–13.

MOORMAN, MARY, *William Wordsworth: A Biography* (2 vols.; Oxford: Clarendon, 1957, 1965).

MUDGE, BRADFORD, *Sara Coleridge: A Victorian Daughter* (London and New Haven: Yale University Press, 1989).

National Portrait Gallery Archive, London, Notes on Collections.

O'DONAGHUE, FREEMAN, *Catalogue of Engraved British Portraits Preserved in the Department of Prints and Drawings in the British Museum* (6 vols.; London: British Museum, 1908–25).

ORMOND, RICHARD, *Daniel Maclise*, exhibition catalogue (London: Arts Council, 1972).

ORMOND, RICHARD, and ROGERS, MALCOLM, *Dictionary of British Portraiture* (4 vols.; New York: Oxford Univeristy Press, 1979).

OSBORNE, HAROLD, *The Oxford Companion to Art* (Oxford: Clarendon, 1970).

PALEY, MORTON D., *Coleridge's Later Poetry* (Oxford: Clarendon, 1996).
—— Coleridge's *'To Matilda Betham, from a Stranger', The Wordsworth Circle*, 27 (1996), 169–72.
—— 'John Camden Hotten and the First British Editions of Walt Whitman—"A Nice Milky Cocoa-Nut" ', *Publishing History*, 6 (1979), 5–36.
PARSON, DONALD, *Portraits of Keats* (Cleveland and New York: World, 1954).
PHILLIPS, THOMAS, Sitters Book, National Portrait Gallery Archive.
PICHOT, AMÉDÉE, *Voyage historique en Angleterre* (2 vols.; Paris: Saunders & Ottley, 1825).
PIPER, DAVID, *The English Face*, 2nd edn. (London: National Portrait Gallery, 1992).
—— *The Image of the Poet: British Poets and Their Portraits* (Oxford: Clarendon, 1982).
PITHEY, WENSLEY, 'A German Coleridge Portrait', *TLS* (1935), 76.
POINTON, MARCIA, *Hanging the Head: Portraiture and Social Formation in Eighteenth-Century England* (New Heaven: Yale University Press, 1993).
RAY, CHARLOTTE WALTERS, 'A Catalogue and Index of the Letters to Ernest Hartley Coleridge', Ph.D. diss., University of Texas at Austin, 1971.
REDGRAVE, RICHARD and SAMUEL, *A Century of British Painters* (Ithaca, NY: Cornell University Press, 1981).
REED, HENRY, MS letters, Historical Society of Pennsylvania.
REED, MARK, *Wordsworth: The Chronology of the Middle Years 1800–1815* (Cambridge, Mass.: Harvard University Press, 1975).
RICHARDSON, EDGAR PRESTON, *Washington Allston: A Study of the Romantic Artist in America* (Chicago: University of Chicago Press, 1948).
ROBINSON, HENRY CRABB, *Diary, Reminiscences, and Correspondence of Henry Crabb Robinson*, ed. Thomas Sadler (3 vols.; London: Macmillan, 1869).
—— *Diary, Reminiscences, and Correspondence of Henry Crabb Robinson*, ed. Thomas Sadler, 3rd edn. (2 vols.; London: Macmillan, 1872).
—— *Henry Crabb Robinson on Books and Their Writers*, ed. Edith J. Morley (3 vols.; London: J. M. Dent, 1938).
Royal Academy, London, Exhibition Catalogues.
Royal Albert Memorial Museum, Exeter, Catalogue, Centenary Exhibition Organized by the University College of the South West of England, Preface by Humphrey House, July–Oct. 1934.

SANDERSON, KENNETH, 'Engravings After Andrew Geddes', *Print Collectors Quarterly*, 16 (1929), 109–31.

SANDFORD, M. E., *Thomas Poole and His Friends* (2 vols.; London and New York: Macmillan, 1888).

—— *Thomas Poole and His Friends* (Over Stowey, Somerset: Friarn, 1996).

SEWTER, A. C., 'Coleridge, Beaumont, and Coleorton', *Leicester and Rutland Magazine*, 1 (1948), 30–5.

SHAKESPEARE, WILLIAM, *The Complete Works of Shakespeare*, ed. Hardin Craig (Chicago: Scott, Foresman, 1951).

SHELLEY, PERCY BYSSHE, *Shelley's Poetry and Prose*, ed. Donald Reiman and Sharon Powers (New York: W. W. Norton, 1977).

Sotheby's *English Literature and History*, sale catalogue, Dec. 1995, no. LN5449.

Sotheby, Wilkinson, and Hodge, *Catalogue of the Well-Known and Valuable Collection of Plumbago, Pen and Ink, and Coloured Pencil Drawings and Miniatures*, London, 18–22 June 1920.

SOUTHEY, ROBERT, *The Life and Correspondence of Robert Southey*, ed. his son, the Revd Charles Cuthbert Southey (6 vols.; London: Longman, Brown, Green, & Longman, 1849–50).

—— *Selections from the Letters of Robert Southey*, ed. John Wood Warter (4 vols.; London: Longman, Brown, Green, & Longman, 1856).

SPURZHEIM, J. G., MD, *The Physiognomical System of Drs. Gall and Spurzheim*, 2nd edn. (London: Baldwin, 1815).

STANLEY, ARTHUR PENRHYN, *Historical Memorials of Westminster Abbey*, 5th edn. (London: John Murray, 1882).

STANNUS, HUGH, 'The Vanguard of the Age', *The Architect: A Weekly Illustrated Journal of Art, Civil Engineering, and Building*, 37 (Jan.–June 1887), 9–10, 23–4, 35; 'The Armitage Frieze', 42–4.

STEVENS, WALLACE, *The Necessary Angel* (London: Faber & Faber, 1959).

STODDARD, RICHARD HENRY (ed.), *Personal Reminiscences by Chorley, Planché, and Young* (New York: Scribner, Armstrong, 1875).

SWEETSER, M. F., *Allston* (Boston: Houghton, Osgood, 1879).

SULTANA, DONALD, *Samuel Taylor Coleridge in Malta and Italy* (Oxford: Basil Blackwell, 1969).

SUNDERLAND, JOHN, *John Hamilton Mortimer: His Life and Works* (London: The Walpole Society, 1988).

THRALL, MIRIAM M. H., *Rebellious Fraser's: Nol Yorke's Magazine in the Days of Maginn, Thackeray, and Carlyle* (New York: Columbia University Press, 1934).

TOLSON, RICHARD, MS memorandum, Highgate Literary and Scientific Institution.

TURNER, JANE (ed.), *The Dictionary of Art* (34 vols.; New York: Grove, 1996).

VOLLMER, HANS (ed.), *Allgemeines Lexicon der Bildenden Kuenstler* [Thieme-Becker] (Leipzig: E. A. Seeman, 1927), xx.

WAKEMAN, GEOFFREY, *Victorian Book Illustration: The Technical Revolution* (Newton Abbot: David & Charles, 1973).

WALKER, ERIC, 'Reading Proof, *Aids to Reflection*, and Phrenology: A New Coleridge Letter', *European Romantic Review*, 8/3 (1997), 323–40.

WALKER, RICHARD, *Regency Portraits* (2 vols.; London: National Portrait Gallery, 1985).

WARD, AILEEN, *John Keats: The Making of a Poet* (New York: Viking, 1963).

WATERHOUSE, ELLIS, *The Dictionary of British Eighteenth Century Painters in Oils and Crayons* (Woodbridge: Antique Collectors' Club, 1981).

WATSON, LUCY, *Coleridge at Highgate* (London: Longmans, Green, 1925).

WHITE, NEWMAN IVEY, *Shelley* (2 vols.; New York: Alfred A. Knopf, 1940).

WHITLEY, WILLIAM T., *Art in England 1800–1820* (Cambridge: Cambridge University Press, 1928).

—— *Artists and Their Friends in England 1700–1799* (London and Boston: Medici Society, 1928).

WARREN, J. COLLINS, MD, 'The Collection of the Boston Phrenological Society—A Retrospect', *Annals of Medical History*, 3 (1921), 1–11.

WILLIAMSON, DR G. C., 'Mr. Francis Wellesley's Collection of Miniatures and Drawings', pt. 1, *The Connoisseur*, 60 (June 1918), 63–75.

WOOLNER, AMY, *Thomas Woolner, R. A.* (London: Chapman and Hall, 1917).

WORDSWORTH, JONATHAN, JAYE, MICHAEL C., and WOOF, ROBERT, *William Wordsworth and the Age of English Romanticism* (New Brunswick and London: Rutgers University Press, 1987).

WORDSWORTH, WILLIAM, *Poems, in Two Volumes, and Other Poems, 1800–1807*, ed. Jared B. Curtis (Ithaca, NY: Cornell University Press, 1983).

—— *The Poetical Works of William Wordsworth*, ed. E. de Selincourt, 2nd edn. (5 vols.; Oxford: Clarendon, 1952), v.

WORDSWORTH, WILLIAM, and WORDSWORTH, DOROTHY, *Letters*, ed. E. de Selincourt, i. *The Early Years 1787–1805*, rev. Chester L. Shaver, 2nd edn. (Oxford: Clarendon Press, 1967).

—— ii. *The Middle Years: Part I, 1806–11*, rev. Mary Moorman, 2nd edn. (Oxford: Clarendon, 1969).
—— vii. *The Later Years: Part 4, 1840–1853*, rev. Alan G. Hill, 2nd edn. (Oxford: Clarendon, 1988).
—— *A Supplement of New Letters*, ed. Alan G. Hill (Oxford: Clarendon, 1993).

Index

Boldface indicates an illustration.